D1617045

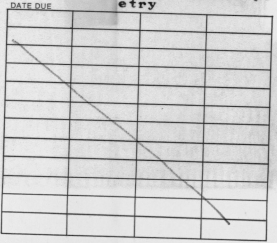

An Anthology of
Modern Arabic Poetry

Selected, Edited and Translated by

MOUNAH A. KHOURI
and
HAMID ALGAR

University of California Press
Berkeley, Los Angeles, London

University of California Press
Berkeley and Los Angeles, California
University of California Press, Ltd.
London, England
Copyright © 1974, by
The Regents of the University of California
ISBN: 0–520–02234–3
Library of Congress Catalog Card Number: 77–189220
Printed in the United States of America

To the memory
of Tawfīq Ṣāyigh

Contents

vii

viii

Preface

With one exception this anthology of eighty poems by thirty-five poets is the sole bilingual collection of modern Arabic poetry attempted to the present. Therefore it fulfills the need for a comprehensive introduction to the subject. The late A. J. Arberry published in 1958 a collection entitled *Modern Arabic Poetry: An Anthology with English Verse Translations*, which covered the period between approximately 1920 and 1945, and which is now considerably out of date. The usefulness of Arberry's anthology is further limited by its exclusion of poets adhering to the free verse movement and by its striving for a geographical completeness of representation. By contrast, the present anthology deals with numerous contemporary poets and contains examples of some of their most recent work, and is moreover characterized by an emphatic concern with the poets of free verse. The neo-classicists have been deliberately omitted as standing outside the modern development; instead, three successive generations of poets have been presented: the Syro-Americans, the Egyptian modernists, and the poets of the free verse movement. These three generations are linked by a progressive shift from emphasis on form to emphasis on content, or, more precisely, from mere portrayal of the external world of the poet to the transmission of the poet's reaction to that world and his vision of it. While it is hoped that the anthology, in view of its bilingual character, will lend itself to use as a textbook, the compilers do not intend that it be exclusively destined for specialists and would be gratified if it reached a wider audience interested in Arabic literature.

As is inevitably the case with the compilation of anthologies, a certain arbitrariness will be apparent in this selection of poems and translations. The range of poets and works chosen is wide enough to represent all important figures, but within this range, taste and predilection operated perforce in the process of selection. An important criterion of choice was the viability of a poem, in its English translation, as a piece of literature, as well as the excellence of its Arabic original. The translation is in all cases as close to the meaning and wording of the original as aesthetic, idiomatic and stylistic considerations permit. With few exceptions, only entire poems have been translated; those offered in extract comprise, it is believed, a unity in themselves.

We should like to thank the al-Khāl Brothers of Beirut, Lebanon, for the skill with which they set the Arabic portion of the text.

The translations are the work of the editors of the anthology unless otherwise indicated in the Biographical Notes.

M.A.K. and H.A.

Introduction

This bilingual anthology offers the reader a unique opportunity to appreciate the poetry of the last three generations of modern Arab poets. Their major works, produced in North and South America and in the Arab world during the last fifty years, are high points in contemporary Arabic verse. Without underestimating the vital contributions of the neo-classical revivalists to the renaissance of Arabic letters, we have centered our attention on the poetical productions of the more recent modernists. Special emphasis is placed on the poets of the free verse movement who are more representative of the radical changes in the nature and function of Arabic poetry and more expressive of the individual experience, vision and mode of existence of the new Arab poet.

Prior to this renaissance, there was a long period of literary decay and stagnation between the Mongols' destruction of the Abbasid dynasty in the thirteenth century and the emergence of Muhammad Ali's Egypt as an independent state within the Ottoman Empire in the nineteenth century. With the exception of a few outstanding writers, this time was marked by an absence of those creative institutions, minds and exceptional individual talents which had produced the great tradition of classical Arabic poetry—the odes and chants of pre-Islamic Arabia, the religious, political, and amatory compositions of the early Umayyad poets, the lyrics of the Andalusians, the mystical poetry of the Sufis and the great classics of the Abbasids. It was not until the latter half of the nineteenth century that Arabic poetry, along with other forms of Arabic literature, began to revive gradually in response to the stimulus of internal reform and the challenge of Western influence.

1

The scholarly literature dealing wholly or in part with this literary renaissance through its various phases prior to the rise of the free verse movement in the 1940's is by now fairly extensive.[1] However, it has barely investigated the true nature of the free verse trend or assessed its contribution to the modernization of Arabic poetry. Within this introduction we propose, therefore, merely to touch on the achievement of the modernizing movements which paved the way for the emergence of the free verse school of poetry, in order to provide a more comprehensive assessment of this new movement and the contributions of its leading poets.

Throughout the eighteenth century concerned Muslims were disturbed by the stagnation of Islamic society within the Ottoman Empire and felt a great need for reform. In the Arabic-speaking world, a few religious leaders made serious efforts to rebuild the Islamic community on the basis of a fresh return and faithful obedience to Islamic law and its ethic. The most important harbinger of Islamic renewal was the Wahhabis of eighteenth-century Arabia. Aiming at a revival of what they considered the true Islam of the pious forerunners (al-Salaf al-Ṣāliḥ), the Wahhabis, by their preaching and implementation of a vigorous, puritanical doctrine inspired by the Ḥanbalī school, and by claiming that their message was the only means of correcting the ills of their society, did indeed constitute a serious challenge to the social and religious conditions in a great portion of the Ottoman Empire. The rise of the Sanūsī order in North Africa later in the century marked another sign of revival from within Islam.

Despite the significance of these and other revivalist movements within the Empire as potent expressions of the growing protest against critical social conditions, none could solve the problems of internal decay and foreign domination confronting the Muslim world by the end of the eighteenth century.

The Napoleonic invasion of Egypt in 1798, however, marked the beginning of a new era of Western intrusion into the Arab Muslim world and was the ancestor of the process of modernization with both its problems and its achievements. With the West sometimes hated as a menace and sometimes admired as a model,

[1] See Bibliography at end of this collection.

2

but constantly present in the minds of the Arabs even to the present time, this process involved a series of radical transformations in the political, social, and cultural conditions of the Arab world.

Among the specific forces of change in this period prior to the Second World War were the spread of education and subsequent increase in literacy, the growth of printing presses and journalism, the production of massive translations and adaptations from Western works, the growing influence of English and French liberal thought on Arabic writers, the emergence of a stream of Islamic thought aimed at restating the social principles of Islam, and the rise of nationalistic movements concerned with the separation of religion from politics and the creation of a secular society. At the end of the Second World War, a great paradox appeared and became quite evident after the Palestine disaster and the creation of a Jewish state in 1948. Differences between the Arabs and the West deepened and multiplied, resulting in a series of revolutions aimed at complete political emancipation from Western domination; yet, unconsciously or by design, contemporary Arabic thought and literature were increasingly subject during this same post-war period to a mounting impact from the West. As a result of this paradox, new movements sprang up not only in politics but also in poetry, fiction, criticism and the other arts.

Among the arts practiced by the Arabs throughout their history, from the pre-Islamic period to the present, non seems to surpass nor even to equal the art of poetry as the ultimate repository of aesthetic awareness. Obsessed by the love of a concise, precise, poetic language, intended for centuries to be orally composed and transmitted through several sets of quantitative monorhymed meters, and designed primarily to produce its evocative effect through the ears of its listeners rather than their eyes, the majority of Arab poets have always been preoccupied with formal perfection as a fundamental norm which largely determines the true value of a poetic creation. Nevertheless, the supreme formal quality as a mark of power in poetical composition and of delight and exultation in aesthetic appreciation has never reduced classical Arabic poetry to an abstract verbal art intended for its own sake and devoid of any social function. On the contrary, if we review the classical poetic tradition, we realize that it has rarely relin-

3

quished its vital role as a vehicle for the portrayal and articulation of the social and intellectual trends of the time. One of the basic concepts of traditional Arabic poetry described its function as "the register (*dīwān*) of the Arabs . . . and their versified discourse, the recorder of their battles, and the witness to their judgements."[2] In early periods poetry was the embodiment of the ancient tradition passed on to future generations. It was this social function of classical poetry in particular which gave rise to its major *aghrāḍ* (aims), such as *madīḥ* (panegyric), *hijā'* (satire), *nasīb* or *ghazal* (love poetry) and *waṣf* (description). Underlying these lyric forms is the classical definition of poetry as "metrical, rhymed speed indicating a meaning."[3] To illustrate this definition, classical critics divided poetry into four constituents, each of which could be criticized independently: word and meaning; word and meter; meaning and meter; and meaning and rhyme. Although of the four elements meter was considered most important for distinguishing poetry from prose, the ideal balance between a beautiful form and an excellent meaning in poetic performance was awarded, in theory as well as in practice, a high mark of excellence.

In addition to this basic criterion which has been retained by prominent poets throughout the literary history of the Arabs, coordination and integration of the various themes within the *qaṣīda* (poem) were also commended by classical critics.[4] However, this unity most frequently pertained to style and composition and involved harmonious and coherent construction of language. It had little relation to the concept of organic unity as developed by Aristotle and revealed in modern poetry. The unity of the traditional *qaṣīda* was psychological and poetic rather than organic. Apart from a strict quantitative meter, the links between the lines of a poem are the experiences held in common by poet and listener. Moreover, the power of the poem lies in its directness and expressiveness of things seen and observed more in the outside world than in the poet's own subjective visions.

Over the period of literary stagnation and into the late nineteenth century, most of these traditional concepts of poetry were

---

[2] Ibn ʿAbd Rabbih, *Kitāb al-ʿIqd al-Farīd* (Cairo, 1940–1965), V, 269.
[3] Qudāmah ibn Jaʿfar, *Naqd al-Shiʿr* (Leiden, 1956), p. 2.
[4] Ibn Ṭabāṭabā, *ʿIyār al-shiʿr* (Cairo, 1956), pp. 124–127.

completely destroyed, especially the preservation of the fundamental balance between form and content and the vital relationship between the "word" of the poet and his "world." The growing tendency toward formalization and artificiality of the poetic art, as developed by imitators and composers of occasional pieces which were cramped with perplexing obscurities, verbal jugglery and false archaism, deprived Arabic poetry of the depth, coherence, and vitality it had had in the preceding centuries and reduced it to a merely ceremonial and for the most part negligible function.

It is within the context of this depleted literary legacy that the formidable task undertaken by the precursors of the renaissance of modern Arabic poetry can best be appreciated and reassessed. In a living, healthy national culture, there is always an interrelationship between all spheres of human activity and a continuous reciprocal influence and interaction of each part of society upon the others. Historically, then, the literary efforts, aims, and achievements of these precursors cannot be isolated from those of the contemporary Muslim thinkers who led one of the most significant reformist movements in modern Islam. In their common pursuit of reform, Maḥmūd Sāmī al-Bārūdī, with whom the modern renaissance truly begins, and Muḥammad ʿAbduh, his friend, seem to follow the same pattern of action. One of ʿAbduh's proclaimed aims was "to liberate thought from the shackles of *taqlīd* (the imitation of established practice) and understand religion as it was understood by the elders of the community before dissension appeared; to return, in the acquisition of religious knowledge, to its first sources, and to weigh them in the scales of human reason." Another of his purposes was "the reform of the way of writing the Arabic language." Committed mainly to the cause of literary reform, al-Bārūdī's task involved, like ʿAbduh's, two major goals: first, to free the poetry prevalent in his time from its artificiality and false archaism, and to turn, in the acquisition of a genuine poetic taste, not to Western literature of which he was totally ignorant, but to the great poetry of the Abbasids and the rich classical Arabic tradition in which he was deeply rooted. Consequently, it was natural that al-Bārūdī's poetry and, to a varying degree, that of the younger generation of poets led by Aḥmad Shawqī and associated with the names of Ḥāfiẓ

5

Ibrāhīm in Egypt, Jamīl Ṣidqī al-Zahāwī, Maʿruf al-Ruṣāfī and Muḥammad Mahdī al-Jawāhirī in Iraq, and Bishāra al-Khūrī in Lebanon, were neo-classical in spirit and execution.

It is true that the classical traditions which directly or indirectly inspired their works far outweighed any Western literary influences. It is also true that the wordiness and poetic diction of their compositions were sometimes a continuation of a scholastic tradition in which philological erudition tended to be of superior urgency to private visions, and that a great deal of their poetry remained sonorous, declamatory, oratorical rather than intimate or lyrical. Nevertheless, with their relatively imposing standards of "good sense," "refinement," and "correctness" in structure and style, and their tendency toward an emotional expression of patriotic and social themes, these poets undoubtedly revived a petrified poetic language, revitalized a dying aesthetic sensibility, reached a wider range of the general public, and achieved in a substantial part of their poetry an authentic expression of current ideas and aspirations.

It is generally agreed that, in the sphere of literary history, each age has its sensibility and its expectation with regard to poetry, and that poetry is the human gesture which is most certain to change as sensibility changes.[5] Moreover, the literature of a given period is not identified merely by the set of existing literary works, but also and equally, by the set of existing literary values. Contemporary norms are the foundation for the valuation of new literary works. From the developmental standpoint, there is always a certain parallel or interrelationship between the historical succession of norms and that of literary works. Yet the two successions cannot always be identified; a certain dynamic antimony from which the literary works derive all the variety of their life may exist between work and norm. This tension can be observed when literary development runs ahead of literary taste, or in the opposite case, when the critics, acting as the carriers of the literary norms, set forth requirements which are only afterwards met by literary creation. It may also be observed when a literary theory exists as a quo norm, without having as its context an existing literary reality.

[5] Archibald MacLeish, *Poetry and Opinion* (Urbana, 1950), p. 38.

6

These concepts are important in any study of the changes in modern Arabic poetry. They are revealed in this collection in poems chosen from the works of the modern poets who succeeded the neo-classicists and who were engaged with them, as well as among themselves, in a creative antimony.

The first major change manifested itself in the poetry of the Lebanese-Egyptian poet Khalīl Muṭrān, whose individual talent and solid training in both classical Arabic tradition and French letters and culture combined to inspire his innovations and qualify him for the decisive role he played in modernizing Arabic poetry. Like Shawqī and other contemporaries, Muṭrān was able to create a new poetic style characterized by its refinement, correctness and classical purity. But unlike their poetry, the best of his compositions reveal distinctive concepts and values never before adopted. Among these were his concern with the principles of organic unity and contextual structure in a poem, as well as his tendency to be moderately lyrical, individualistic, introspective and expressive of his private vision. Armed with his notion of poetry as a conscious art, he rejected the extreme form of neo-classic rationalism and moved in his poetry toward a stronger emotional conception of taste. Under the direct influence of the French romantics, particularly Hugo's poetic narratives, Musset's lyrics, and Baudelaire's *Les Fleurs du Mal*, he developed in a significant part of his work the first romantic trend in contemporary Arabic verse.

Focussing in his poetry on the primacy of meaning, Muṭrān attacked despotism, tyranny, class distinction, ignorance, and social injustice and championed the cause of progress, national freedom and liberal thought in his age.

In view of his deep concern with the principle of organic unity which determines the internal coordination and emerging unity of texture in a poetical composition, he became fully aware of the severe limitations of the Arabic prosodic system. In order to pinpoint these limitations, he ventured to create the longest poem of its kind in the history of Arab letters. In the introduction to his four-hundred line, epic-like, monometered, monorhymed poem called *Nayrūn* (Nero), Muṭrān explained the nature and value of this composition:

7

Until today, Arabic poetry has not included great long poems dealing with a single topic, because the use of one monorhyme throughout the poem was, and still is, an obstacle to any such attempt. I wanted to discover, through my own conclusive efforts, the utmost limits a poet could reach in the composition of a long poem dealing with one subject and using monorhyme. Once I had reached those limits in my poetic experimentation, I would then be able to show my fellow-speakers of Arabic the necessity of following different patterns to achieve the progress which had been attained by Western poetry.[6]

Muṭrān's task, then, was to destroy the *qaṣīda* pattern after exhausting its poetic potentials and to show that it must be replaced by freer and more suitable forms of poetry.

Beyond these significant innovations, which involved a series of breaches with the current neo-classical trend and which advanced Arabic poetry toward a freer language, richer themes, newer forms and techniques, and a more coherent mode of existence, the process of poetic modernization had to be carried out by a younger group of poets.

Partly influenced by Muṭrān and partly by the English romantic poets and critics, particularly Hazlitt and Coleridge, three Egyptian modernists known as the Diwan Group—Shukrī, al-ʿAqqād and al-Māzinī—set out on a new path. Their objective was, in essence, to consolidate the romantic trend generated by Muṭrān which was destined to be reinforced by a similar current being developed simultaneously by their contemporaries, the Mahjar or Syro-American group.

Despite differences in character and temperament which, among other factors, led to the rift between the Diwan poets, it is quite evident that both al-ʿAqqād and al-Māzinī shared Shukrī's ideas and that their thinking remained within the general framework of his concepts of poetry. Chief among Shukrī's views are the rejection of the unity of the *bayt* (line of verse) and the emphasis on the organic unity of the poem; the insistence on clarity, simplicity, and quiet beauty of the poetic language; and the necessity of drawing upon all sources of inspiration, traditional and foreign, which broaden and deepen the poet's perception and sensibility. But more important than these concepts, already advocated by Muṭrān, was Shukrī's redefinition of poetry as *wijdān* (emotion),

[6] Muṭrān, *Dīwān* (Cairo, 1948–1949), III, p. 50.

in which the emotional conception of taste becomes a decisive factor in determining the true nature and function of poetry; this marked a positive departure from the neo-classical tradition to a new era of romanticism in contemporary Arabic poetry.

Shukrī's early collections of poetry emphasize the need for social change and reveal his faith in scientific progress and rationalism. In his later poetry two main themes may be discerned: a reflection on life with its evils and sufferings and, at the same time, a submission to that life in the belief that a sensibility which would enjoy the true, the beautiful, and the good could not avoid exposing itself to the malaise beneath which they are submerged. In addition, his own misfortunes and those of his country combined to suffuse his poetry with dark pessimism.

Shukrī's contribution and that of the Diwan school to the development of new concepts of poetry cannot be exaggerated. Their norms reveal a sophisticated insight into the nature and distinctive features of English romanticism, and constitute the first challenging attempt to displace the norms of the neo-classical school from their firmly-established position. However, due to a striking discrepancy between the high level of their conceptual schemes and poetic ideals, and the mediocrity of their actual poetic performance, it was more as critics than as poets that they made a significant change in the current of literary appreciation.

What the Egyptian modernists were doing during the second and third decades of this century was also being done in North and, to a lesser extent, South America by the Mahjar poets and critics, who successfully transformed their new prescriptive norms into an impressive literary reality and exercised through their creative writings a greater influence upon Arabic letters. These Mahjar poets came from among the Syrian and Lebanese emigrants who left their homeland for America in search of material prosperity and political freedom.

Although the conditions of the early Arab emigrants were marked by hardship and insecurity, they eventually achieved some degree of success in the various aspects of their new life abroad. Culturally, they were caught between two traditions—a Western tradition exercising a direct influence on their minds and attitudes, and an Arab tradition which they tried to preserve and modernize. In an effort to carry out this latter task they

9

published their own newspapers, journals and works, and founded various social and literary organizations which contributed to their cultural activity. The most important literary societies were al-Rābiṭah al-Qalamīyah (The Pen League) founded in New York in 1920 (with Gibrān as its president, Nuʿaymah as its secretary, ʿArīḍa, Ayyūb, and the Ḥaddād brothers and others as its members), and al-ʿUṣbah al-Andalusīyah (The Andalusian League) founded in São Paulo and associated with the names of Fawzī and Shafīq al-Maʿlūf, Ilyās Farḥāt, Rashīd S. al-Khūrī and others. These poets of the South American Mahjar produced excellent poetry inspired in some aspects of its forms and themes by the Andalusian lyrics and revealing a great deal of originality. In general, however, they remained much more conservative in their innovations than their compatriots in North America.

Many factors combined to give the northern Mahjar literature a distinctive character. Living in a totally Western environment and feeling a compelling need for the expression of ideas and experiences arising from their new conditions of life, educated during their formative years in Western-oriented missionary schools in Syria or Lebanon with a greater exposure to Western thought and literature than to their own culture, and removed after their emigration to the New World from the strains and doubts which assailed fellow-Arabs in their homeland, the North American Mahjar writers were much more prepared than any of their contemporaries to play a decisive role in revitalizing Arabic letters and shaping Arab sensibility.

In general, their ideas may be characterized as romantic, humanistic, and often mystical. They shared the belief that they lived in an age with its own sensibility and its own expectation of literature and its function. They agreed on the need for adopting a new concept of language, neither sacred nor profane but rather a living medium of expression subject to changes and developments. Consequently, they emphasized the need for reviving the Arabic language and restoring to it the simplicity and vitality that centuries of stagnant conservatism had destroyed. In addition, they stressed human experience and subjective feeling as the basis and source of all true literature.

The better-educated writers from among the northern group, Gibrān, Nuʿaymah and al-Rīḥānī, were in general influenced by the romantic literature of the West, by the American transcendentalists, especially Emerson, and by such poets as Longfellow, Whittier, and Whitman. Apart from a common background, experience, literary taste and the pursuit of common objectives, they had no specific ideology and showed in their works various individual tendencies.

It is generally agreed that Gibrān was the leading and most influential figure of the Mahjar writers. His work is colored by an overwhelming *mal de siècle*, a revolt against the established modes of thought in social, religious and literary spheres. Having been uprooted by emigration, Gibrān was nurtured by Western ideas and influences such as those of Nietzsche, Blake, Rodin, the romanticism and transcendentalism of American literature, and the Bible, as well as by recollections of Eastern mysticism; he produced works, both literary and artistic, permeated by feelings of exile and nostalgia for his native land, of yearning to return to nature and seek lost innocence and pure love, and by a kind of metaphysical melancholy and vague pseudo-mysticism. The difficulties of form were resolved by the new style he created in his poetic prose and prose poems, which proved to be a milestone in the history not only of Arabic poetry but of Arabic letters generally.

Nuʿaymah, in his critical writing and later in his poetry, plays, novels, short stories and philosophical essays, embraced Gibrān's basic premises and ideals. He reformulated them clearly and accurately, and reinforced their liberating and salutary effect on the modern trend in Arabic literature. No less important is the influence of Amīn al-Rīhānī, who throughout his career saw himself as a connecting link between East and West, trying to bring the "spirituality" of the East to the West and the progressiveness of the West to the East. A realist at heart, he was much more concerned than Gibrān, Nuʿaymah, and the other Mahjar writers with solutions to the political, social and cultural problems of the Arab world, and he called for a literary revolution as an adjunct to the general Arab awakening which he advocated.

In his view, literary modernism must encompass the spirit and total outlook of the creative effort. The literary modernizer must find or create a style in harmony with his sensibility and view of life. In his effort to actualize this concept, and under the

11

influence of the Koranic style and of Whitman's mode of expression, al-Rīhānī created the first consciously conceived model of prose poetry (al-shi'r al-manthūr) in Arabic. He attempted in this experiment to develop a new form, free from prosodic literary bonds and capable of expressing the ideas and feelings of the modern poet in a more suitable form and language.[7]

Two other outstanding poets of the Syro-American group should be mentioned. Īliyā Abū Māḍī distinguished himself among the northern Mahjaris by his lyrical outpourings which expressed skepticism and questioning of the established social and ethical norms. Fawzī al-Ma'lūf, from among the southern Mahjaris, is famous for his elegantly polished, long poem, 'Alā Bisāt al-Rīh (On the Carpet of the Wind), in which he expressed a private vision of his wretched existence and his soul's yearning in an ethereal world of his own imagining for its lost freedom and purity.

Despite the attempts of the traditionalists to curb the vogue of the Mahjar romantic movement, these leading figures remained the principal representatives of the new Arabic literature and their works served as a source of inspiration for the following generation of Arab poets.

Romanticism, as developed by the Diwan school and more effectively promoted by Gibrān and the Mahjar poets, reached its height in the Arab world in the 1930's. The presence of the French in Syria, Lebanon and North Africa, and of the British in Egypt, Iraq and Palestine, suppressed the struggle of these countries for complete independence, and frustrated their national hopes and aspirations. This situation produced a general climate of disillusionment, malaise, pessimism and despair which was closely reflected in the romantic writings of the Arab poets. The important romantic poets at this time were those with the Apollo magazine founded by Ahmad Zakī Abū Shādī in Egypt in 1932, and including 'Alī Mahmūd Tahā, Ibrāhīm Nājī and the Tunisian Abū al-Qāsim al-Shābbī whose romantic subjectivism stands in sharp contrast to the formal neo-classicism of Shawqī's followers and is most reflective of a generation in torment. In Syria, romanticism was partly echoed in 'Umar Abū Rīsha's poetry, while in Lebanon it found articulate expression in the poetry of

[7] al-Rīhānī, "al-Shi'r al-Manthūr," Adab wa fann (Beirut, 1957), p. 45.

12

Ilyās Abū Shabakah. Deeply rooted in the Christian tradition of the Maronite sector of the Lebanese community and thoroughly educated at the local French missionary schools in French literary and cultural tradition, with special attraction to Baudelaire's poetry, Abū Shabakah reveals in his poetical compositions a depth of subjective experience and searching introspection rarely achieved before.

With the Second World War over, a new era began in the Arab world characterized by a significant transformation in the social and political life of Arab society. In conjunction with the struggle for self-government, there grew up a number of political parties aimed not only at achieving independence from foreign domination but also at preserving and consolidating such independence on the basis of a political doctrine and a specific program of social and economic reform. Anṭūn Saʿādah's Social Nationalist Party played a leading part in the affairs of both Lebanon and Syria in the 1940's; the Baʿth Party became all-powerful in Iraq and Syria and was eventually largely responsible for the formation of the United Arab Republic in 1958; the Muslim Brothers' Society was influential in the religious, social and political affairs of Egypt between 1945 and 1954; the Communist Party grew in Syria and Iraq; and there was a rising tide of Arab nationalism throughout the Arab world. Despite basic divergences in their aims and principles, these parties created within the various sectors of Arab society a strong motivation for establishing a new order and engaged their followers in conscious militant action against internal corruption and foreign domination. As a result of this dynamic atmosphere in which many intellectuals were deeply involved, a new sense of commitment to the cause of national freedom and the reorganization of Arab society manifested itself in the early socio-political poetry of a number of young poets such as ʿAlī Aḥmad Saʿīd (Adonis), the voice of the Social Nationalist Party in Syria and Lebanon, and al-Sayyāb and al-Bayātī, spokesman for the Iraqi Communist Party.

The Palestine tragedy in 1948, with its repercussions in the Arab world, proved to be a turning point in the modern history of the Arabs, both politically and culturally. In reaction to that disaster one revolution after another swept most of the traditional regimes in the Arab world; in the literary sphere, a vigorous effort to give point to the nation's wrath and suffering, to crystallize its new mode of thought and expression, and to stimulate its fresh hopes and aspirations, resulted in the rejection of the existent poetic trends and in the creation of yet another type of poetry that revolutionized the whole nature and function of modern Arabic verse.

Already by 1945, romanticism and the symbolist movement led in the late thirties, under the impact of French symbolism, by the Lebanese poets Yūsuf Ghusub, Saʿīd ʿAql and Ṣalāḥ Labakī, were becoming dying techniques. They were completely rejected by the new poets, who believed that the value of poetry lies primarily in its social usefulness. These poets condemned romanticism as a sterile theory of art destined to produce an idle, gloomy and self-centered type of poetry. They attacked symbolism as a display of ingenious contrivances of art-for-art's-sake, insignificant in human life. The new force called in to replace these trends was the free verse movement which altered the total picture of poetic tradition and illustrated further the direction in which modern Arabic poetry is going and where it can go.

How did this free verse movement rise? Are its literary concepts, as some critics believe, the historically-determined product of the social changes which occurred in the Arab world? Or are they, as others assert, merely a reproduction of Western poetical norms and techniques? What are the distinguishing features of this new type of Arabic poetry?

Some aspects of free verse may be found in the few "prose poems" of Gibrān and al-Rīhānī, the "blank verse" of al-Zahāwī, Shukrī and Bā Kathīr. However, all these compositions were basically isolated experiments with little bearing on the emergence of free verse as it developed more consciously at the hands of its first serious pioneer, Lewis ʿAwaḍ.[8]

In his collection entitled *Plutoland and Other Poems from the Poetry of the Elite*, ʿAwaḍ illustrated both theoretically and in practice the basic poetic norms and patterns which characterized the free verse movement. His book was published in Cairo in 1947 and consists of a critical introduction which explains his theories, and of twenty-nine poems dealing with social and individual

[8] Mounah A. Khouri, "Lewis ʿAwaḍ: A Pioneer of the Free Verse Movement," *Journal of Arabic Literature*, Vol. I, 1970.

themes, fourteen of them written in literary Arabic and fifteen in Egyptian colloquial. Five poems of the first group are dated 1938, four 1939, and three 1940. All the poems of the second group are dated 1940. Most of the poems in the collection were composed in Cambridge, England, where ʿAwaḍ was studying.

It is clear from the dates of ʿAwaḍ's poems that they were written several years before al-Malāʾikah and al-Sayyāb wrote their two isolated poems, which appeared in 1947 and which had been considered the earliest compositions of free verse poets. Without overemphasizing the importance of dates in discussing the emergence of a movement whose origins are too complex to be traced to a given point in time and place, still it is evident that historically ʿAwaḍ's work lies at the root of the movement.

In his search for a new vision of poetry, ʿAwaḍ seems to have been guided by the following factors:

1. His consciousness that what distinguishes his age from that of the neo-classic Arab poets is a new sensibility and consequently a new expectation with regard to modern Arabic poetry.

2. His awareness that the prevailing outmoded tradition of Arabic poetry has a chance of tremendous revival if the new poets could appreciate the importance of the modern experiments and discover new directions in poetic development that may be found in Western literary achievements as well as in certain elements of their own literature.

In fact, ʿAwaḍ has rediscovered in the literary history of the Arabs two significant trends: the creation, on the one hand, by the Andalusian poets of a genuine poetry in which the Khalīlī prosodic system was radically altered, but the classical language basically preserved; and, on the other hand, the destruction of both the classical language and the Khalīlī prosodic patterns by the popular poets in Egypt and other Arab lands.

As a comparatist, ʿAwaḍ discovered in Western literature a pattern to guide him in his first experiment. The emergence of a new Italian language, freed from the established norms of Latin, encouraged him to attempt a new quality of vernacular poetry that would not be obscured or ignored by the elite.

The immediate results were the colloquial experiments in his collection. These, ʿAwaḍ says, were greeted with hostility in

Egypt. Among his other experiments one group included examples of three Western genres: narrative (non-epic) poetry, the ballad, and the sonnet. His remaining experiments derive from his westernized conception of poetry and his rejection of the Khalīlī prosodic system as archaic.

Perhaps ʿAwaḍ's most important experiment is his free verse poem "Kiriyalayson" written in Cambridge, England, May 9, 1938. In this poem ʿAwaḍ tries a "pyramidal" pattern beginning with a single tafʿīlah "mustafʿilun" and expanding until it has a large base. Underlying this experiment is the shift from the traditional bayt to the tafʿīlah as the basic unit. This change enabled ʿAwaḍ to vary the length of his lines so that each individual thought or feeling might find its own unique word movement. In principle, this device became a distinguishing feature of the whole group of tafʿīlī poets within the free verse movement.

Although ʿAwaḍ's work must be recognized as the first serious attempt at free verse, it was undoubtedly the Iraqi poetess Nāzik al-Malā'ikah who, first in the introduction to her collection Sha-ẓāyā wa-Ramād and later in her book Qaḍāyā al-Shiʿr al-Muʿāṣir (1962), laid the theoretical foundations for the development of this new form. Al-Malā'ikah was concerned with freeing Arabic poetry from the regularity characteristic of the traditional forms. With the single line of verse as the basic unit of the qaṣīda pattern, the molds of Arabic poetry imposed their form on the content and quite often deprived the resulting poetical composition of its vital effect. Thus al-Malā'ikah advocated the need for a free verse, in which the meter is based upon the unit of the tafʿīlah (foot) and the freedom of the poet is secured through his right to vary the tafʿīlāt (feet) or the lengths of his lines as he feels most appropriate for the expression of his message. However, she limited the range of this freedom by requiring that the tafʿīlāt in the lines be completely similar. This meant that, of the sixteen traditional meters, only seven (Kāmil, Ramal, Hazaj, Rajaz, Mutaqārib, Khafīf and Wāfir), which are based on the repetition of a single tafʿīlah, could be used by the free verse poets. The other meters were considered inappropriate for this type of poetry. Furthermore, al-Malā'ikah insisted on the use of rhyme in free verse for its rhythmical and organizational value in the making of a poem.

These are, in broad lines, al-Malā'ikah's basic principles for the development of free verse. Many poets and critics rejected them on the assumption that they were arbitrary rules no less rigid than those of al-Khalīl's prosodic system. Other poets modified them by using combined meters in their compositions or by inventing their own *tafʿīlāt*. In his criticism of al-Malā'ikah's theories, Muḥammad al-Nuwayhī, a prominent Egyptian critic, advocated the shift of the basis of modern Arabic verse from its traditional quantitative structure to the accentual pattern of English poetry.

Notwithstanding the fact that the quantitative *tafʿīlah* as the basic unit still bound free verse to the traditional poetry, this new form, as successfully used by several outstanding modern poets, marked a significant change in some basic aspects of the Arabic poetic tradition. By relying on the development of internal music, and in transmitting their message to their new, mass audience by use of a freer and simpler mode of expression verging on the form of speech, the free verse poets restored to their art its vitality and its important role in public life. This achievement is evident in the free verse productions of al-Sayyāb, al-Bayāti, ʿAbd al-Ṣabūr, Adonis, Qabbāni, Ḥāwī, Ṭūqān and other poets included in this collection.

Another revolutionary group of poets was simultaneously developing a radically new form of free verse poetry. Rejecting the earlier free verse as still inadequate for the expression of visions and experiences, this group freed itself from all the accepted elements of Arabic poetry such as meter, rhyme, *tafʿīlah* and unit, and ventured to create a truly free and highly personalized form of poetry. Due to the absence of any specific pattern in this freer form of composition it was attacked as "non-poetry" and given, when it first appeared, a variety of names including "verse in prose," "prose poetry," "prose poems," and the like. But it was seldom accepted for what it really is—genuine poetry. A recent investigation of this newer form[9] reveals that, in its formal aspects, it largely follows the general principles which define a prose poem. "The prose poem, not only in form but also in essence, is based on the union of opposites: prose and poetry, freedom and discipline, destructive anarchy and organizing art. . . .

[9] Julie Scott Meisami, "New Forms in Modern Arabic Poetry," Ph.D. Thesis, University of California, Berkeley, 1970.

Hence its inner contradictions; hence its profound dangerous and fertile antinomies; hence its perpetual tension and dynamism."[10] Structurally, Arabic prose poems ranged from highly structured and logically organized compositions to unstructured and anarchical ones. The chief representative of this most recently developed poetic form are Tawfīq Ṣāyigh, Jabrā Ibrāhīm Jabrā, Yūsuf al-Khāl, Adonis, Muḥammad al-Māghūṭ and Unsī al-Ḥājj.

All the poets whose names are associated with the free verse movement, whether in its experimental phase, in its *tafʿīlah* stage or in this latest development, were subject to a mounting impact from the West. It is generally agreed that the foreign influences which left their mark on Arabic letters before 1950 were largely French. But in the early 1950's English and American writers, especially T. S. Eliot, became of major significance for Arabic poetry. In his perceptive assessment of Eliot's deep impact, Jabrā Ibrāhīm Jabrā, a leading poet-critic, says: "T. S. Eliot fascinated many of the new Arab authors because he seemed to be an articulate and concise advocate of their incipient thoughts. . . . The Arab poets responded so passionately to 'The Wasteland' because they, too, went through an experience of universal tragedy, not only in World War II, but also, and more essentially, in the Palestine *débacle* and its aftermath. In this latter, 'The Wasteland' and its implication seemed strangely to fit. A whole order of things has crumbled, and the theme of the parched land waiting for rain; of fertility restored through the blood of Tammuz, murdered by the wild boar; of death and resurrection, never really abandoned our poets."[11]

Jabrā also pointed out how Eliot's view of tradition, as kept alive by the interaction between new and old through individual talent, his forthright use of language with its simple words and great immediacy, his resourceful poetic technique which employed variety and surprise, were partly responsible for the great change in modern Arabic poetry. Needless to say, contemporary Arab poets were also attracted by other Western sources of in-

[10] Suzanne Bernard, *Le Poème en Prose de Baudelaire jusqu'à nos jours*, Paris, 1959, p. 462.

[11] Jabrā Ibrāhīm Jabrā, paper delivered at Oxford, November 1968, and published in *Journal of Arabic Literature*, Vol. I, pp. 83–84, under title of "Modern Arabic Literature and the West."

spiration; Edith Sitwell, Ezra Pound, Pablo Neruda, Mayakovsky, Aragon, Eluard St. John Perse, Sartre, Camus and many others have all had their share of influence.

It must be emphasized, however, that the influence of the West mainly pointed out new directions and awakened poets to new methods, new ideas and new possibilities. Although Arabic poetry has come closer to Western poetry, it has never relinquished its own character or originality. In fact, the modern poets are now writing not only Arabic poems, but also Arab poems. The Western influence, therefore, was not one of enslavement through imitation but rather one of liberation.

In a general sense, it is safe to conclude that the Arab poets of the last two decades have been stimulated by the efforts and achievements of the earlier modernists and have been made conscious of the radical changes which have overtaken all aspects of life in their society. They have responded creatively to the challenging impact of Western culture on their modes of thought and expression, and have produced for the first time in several centuries a most original type of Arabic poetry.

This dynamic form, rejecting the inviolability of traditional metrics and the lifeless poetic diction in favor of a freer, simpler poetic language, is capable of a more vital expression of content through the intensity of the artistic process and the imaginative use of words, metaphors, symbols, imagery, mythological allusions, dramatic monologues and other devices. This content ranges from universal philosophical questions about the human condition, life, death, love, and salvation to the particular social and cultural issues and situations characteristic of the poets' own time, visions and experiences. In their endeavors to pigeonhole the various groups of modern poets, critics have called them romantics, social realists, Eliotists, Tammuzists, existentialists, Palestinian elegists and other names; these descriptions are merely inadequate attempts to tame the rebellious and to represent in straight lines a dynamic poetic current which has numerous curves and divergences. In fact, this poetic energy is characteristic of the nature and function of the new poetry and is commensurate with the sensibility of the composers who, unlike their predecessors, feel that they are one with the complex world and its problems and are thoroughly steeped in the restless spirit of the period in which they live. Existentially they are committed as creative artists to enlarging their fellowman's sensibility, deepening his sympathies, and inducing some order, harmony and vitality in the world around him.

An Anthology of Modern Arabic Poetry

جبران خليل جبران

صوتـان

وانسَّ ما قلتُ وقلتـا	أعطني النـاي وغنِّ
فأدني مـا فعلتـا	إنما النطـقُ هبـاءُ
منزلاً دون القصورْ	هل تخذت الغاب مثلـي
وتسلقت الصخـورْ؟	فتتبعـت السواقـي
وتنشفت بنـورْ	هلى تحممتَ بعطـرٍ
في كؤوس مـن أثيرْ؟	وشربتَ الفجر خمراً
بين جفنات العنـبْ	هل جلست العصر مثلي
كثريـات الذهـبْ	والعناقيـد تدلَّـتْ
ولمن جاع الطعـامْ	فهي للصادي عيون
ولمن شاءَ المـدامْ	وهي شهدٌ وهي عطرٌ
وتلحّفتَّ الفضـا	هل فرشْتَ العشب ليلاً
ناسياً مـا قـد مـضى؟	زاهداً في ما سيأتـي
موجـهُ في مسمعكْ	وسكوت الليل بحـرٌ
خافق في مضجعـكْ	وبصـدر الليل قلبٌ
وانسَّ داءً ودواء	أعطني الناي وغنِّ
كُتبت لكـن بمـاء	إنما الناس سطـورٌ
في اجتماع وزحـام	ليت شعري أيَّ نفعٍ
واحتجـاجٍ وخصامْ؟	وجدالٍ وضجيـج

22

Gibrān Khalīl Gibrān

Two Voices

Give me the flute and sing! Forget all that you and I
    have said;
Talk is but dust in the air, so tell me of your deeds.

Have you, like me, spurned palaces and taken the forest as abode,
Followed the brooks in their courses, climbed the rocks?

Have you bathed in fragrance, dried yourself with light,
Quaffed the wine of dawn from ethereal goblets?

Have you, like me, rested in the evening in the grape arbor,
The clusters hanging down like golden chandeliers?

For the thirsty, they are as springs, for the hungry, as food.
Honey they are, and perfume; and wine for who so wishes.

Have you bedded in the grass at night, with the vast sky for cover,
Unconcerned with what shall come, forgetting what has passed,
While the silence of the night is a sea whose waves echo in your
    ears,
And where you lie beats a heart, in the breast of night?

Give me the flute and sing! Forget distress and cure,
For people are lines which are written not with ink
    but water.
Would that I knew what good there is in throng and crowd,
In strife and clamor, argument and quarrel.

كلها أنفاق خُلـــدٍ   وخيــوط   العنكبــوتْ

فالذي يحيــا بعجــزٍ   فهو في بطءٍ يمــوتْ

العيشُ في الغاب والأَيام لو نُظمت

في قبضتي لغدت في الغاب تنتـــــثرُ

لكن هو الدهرُ في نفسي لـه أربْ

فكلما رمتُ غابـاً قامَ يعتذرُ

وللتقادير سبلٌ لا تغيّرهـــا

والناس في عجزهم عن قصدهم قصروا

أمين الريحاني

دفاعا عن النور

النور ، النور ! ليسطع في قلوبنا ، وان أظلم العالم ، لينتشر من قلوبنا ، وان اكفهرت الآفاق كلها .

فان لم يكن لي غير كوخ في الوادي تنيره في الليل شمعة ناحلة ، فان العين لتعكس في الكوخ ما تراه من انوار العالم .

وان هبت العاصفة فاقتلعت كوخي كما تقتلع الأشجار ، وذهبت به إلى مصب الأنهار ، فهناك كهف في الصخور لا تقوى العواصف عليه ، وهناك نور الشمس ، وهنالك أنوار النجوم .

وأن ادلهمت السماء ، وطمست الكواكب والنجوم ، فها هنا ، في هذا القلب البشري ، النور الخالد .

ليسطع النور في قلوبنا ، وان اكفهرت الآفاق كلها جمعاء .

They all are but the tunnels of moles, threads in the
    spider's web,
For he who lives in weakness, slowly he will die.

Forest is the abode of life, and were the days
    gathered in my hand, there would I strew them,
But Time it is that chooses from my soul; whenever I long
    for forest Time bars my way with excuses;
The Fates have ways unaltering,
    and men's aims are beyond their impotent reach.

Amīn al-Rīḥānī

Light

Light! Light! Let it shine in our hearts, however dark the world
    may be.
Let it flow forth from our hearts, however somber the horizons
    may be.
Though I have only a hut in the valley, lit in the night by a meager
    candle,
my eye reflects in the hut all the light it beholds in the world.
And should the storm blow and uproot my hut as it uproots the
    trees,
carrying it to the river's mouth,
there is a cave there among the rocks impregnable to the storm,
    and there
is the light of the sun and the stars.
And should the heavens darken and the planets and stars be
    eclipsed,
still in this human heart is light eternal.
Let light shine in our hearts, however somber the horizons may be.

ميخائيل نعيمه

أخي

أخي ، إن ضَجَّ بعد الحرب غربيٌّ بأعماله
وقدّسَ ذِكْرَ مَن ماتوا وعظّم بطشَ أبطاله
فلا تَهزج لِمن سادوا ، ولا تشمت بمن دانا
بــل اركع صامتاً مثلي بقلب خاشعٍ دامٍ
لنبكي حظَّ موتانا

[*]

أخي ، إن عاد بعد الحرب جنديٌّ لأوطانه
وألقى جسمَه المنهوكَ في أحضـان خلاّنه ،
فلا تطلب إذا ما عُدتَ للأوطان خلاّنـا
لأنّ الجوع لم يترك لنا صَحباً نناجيهـــمْ
سوى أشباح موتانـا

أخي . إن عاد يحرث أرضَهُ الفلاّحُ أو يزرعْ
ويبني بعد طول الهجر كوخاً هــدّه المدفع
فقد جفّت سواقينـا وهـدّ الذلُّ مأوانا
ولم يترك لنـا الأعداءُ غرساً في أراضينـا
سوى أجياف موتانا

26

Mikhā'īl Nuʿaymah

My Brother

Brother, if after the war the Man of the West
    celebrates his deeds,
Praising the memory of those who died, and
    glorifying the valor of his heroes,
Do not sing for those who have won the day, and
    do not rejoice over the misfortune of those
    who have yielded in surrender;
Rather kneel down in silence, as I do, with humble,
    bleeding heart that we may weep the fate of
    our dead.

Brother, if the soldier after the war comes back
    to his home country
Throwing his exhausted body into the embrace of
    his bosom friends,
Do not ask when you have returned to the home country
    for the bosom friends;
For hunger has left us no friends with whom we may
    speak intimately
    Except the shadows of our dead.

Brother, if the farmer returns to plow his land
    and to sow,
And after long exile to build his cottage which
    the cannon has destroyed;
The water wheels have dried up, humiliation has
    destroyed our shelter.
And the enemy have not left us any seedling on
    our lands
    Other than the corpses of our dead.

أخي ، قد تمّ ما لو لم نشأهُ نحن ما تمّا
وقد عمّ البلاءُ ، ولو أردنا نحن ما عمّا
فلا تندب ، فأذنُ الغير لا تصغي لشكوانا
بل اتبعني لنحفر خندقاً بالرّفش والمعولْ
نواري فيه موتانا
أخي ، من نحن ؟ لا وطنٌ ولا أهلٌ ولا جارُ
إذا نمنا ، إذا قمنا ، ردانا الحزيُ والعارُ
لقد خمّت بنا الدنيا كما خمّت بموتانا .
فهـات الرّفش واتبعني لنحفر خندقاً آخـر
نواري فيه أحيانا ...

أوراق الخريف

تناثـري   تناثري
يـا بهجة النظرْ
يا مرقص الشمس ويا
أرجوحـة   القمـر
يا أرغن الليـل ويـا
قيثـارة السّحَـرْ
يا رمز فكـرٍ حائرٍ
ورسـم روحٍ ثائـرٍ
يا ذكر مجـدٍ غابـرٍ
قـد عافـكَ الشّجرْ
تنـاثري ! تنـاثري !

28

Brother, what has happened never would have come
     about, had we not willed it.
Disaster has become universal, though had we wished,
     it would not have been so.
Do not lament, for no one else will lend an ear
     to our complaints.
Rather follow me that we may dig a trench with
     spade and pick
     In which to hide our dead.

Dear brother, who are we with no country,
     no people, no neighbor?
When we sleep and when we wake, we put on
     shame and dishonor.
The world smells rotten with our stench as
     it has smelled with our dead.
So bring the spade and follow me that we may
     dig another trench
     In which to bury our living.

Autumn Leaves

Scatter! Scatter!
O delight of the eyes!
O dance court of the sun!
And swing of the moon!
O organ of the night!
Guitar of enchantment!
O symbol of bewildered thought!
And image of the rebel soul!
O memory of glory that has passed
Cast off by the trees.
Scatter! Scatter!

وعانقــي تعــانقــي
أشبـــاحَ مــا مَضى
وزوّدي أنظــــارك
مــن طلعــة الفضـا
هيهات أنْ، هيهاتَ أن
يعـــود مـــا انقضى
وبعـدَ أن تفارقـي
أترابَ عهـد سابقِ
سيري بقلبٍ خـافقٍ
في موكـبِ القضـا
تعـانقي ! تعـانقي !

سيري ولا تعـاتبي
لا ينفــع العتــابْ
ولا تلومـي الغصن
والرّيــاح والسّحـاب
فهي إذا خاطبتها
لا تحسن الجــواب
والدّهر ذو العجائب
وباعـث النّـوائبِ
وخانـقُ الرغائبِ
لا يفهــم الخطابْ
سيري ولا تعـاتبي !

عودي إلى حضن الثرى
وجـدّدي العهــودْ
وانسي جمالاً قد ذوى
ما كـان لن يعـود
كم أزهرت من قبلك
وكــم ذوت ورود
فلا تخافي ما جرى

30

Embrace one another and embrace
The shades of what has passed.
Feast your gaze upon
The sight of Space.
Never, oh never
Will what is past return.
And after you have left
The companions of a bygone age,

Proceed with beating heart
In the caravan of Fate.
Embrace one another! Embrace!
Proceed and do not blame,
For blame serves no purpose.
And do not blame the branch
Nor the winds nor the clouds,
For should you speak to them
They would not have the right answer.

Time is full of wonders,
Sending calamities,
And stifling desires;
Fate does not understand your speech,
So proceed along and do not blame.

Go back to the bosom of the earth.
Renew the cycle of ages.
Forget faded beauty.
What has been will not return.

How many roses before you have blossomed
And how many have faded!
Fear not what has happened

ولا تلومـي القَـدَرا
من قد أضاع جوهـرا
يلقــاه في اللّحــودْ
عودي إلى حضن الثّرى !

الطمأنينة

سقفُ بيتي حديــدْ — ركنُ بيتي حجـرْ
فاعـصفي يـا رياحْ — وانتحبْ يا شجرْ
واسبحي يـا غيومْ — واهطـلي بالمطر
واقصفي يـا رعودْ — لست أخشى خطر
سقفُ بيتي حديــدْ — ركن بيتي حجرْ !

من سراجي الضّئيل — أستمدُّ البصرْ
كلّما الليلُ طــالْ — والظّـلام انتشر
وإذا الفجرُ مــاتْ — والنّهارُ انتحرْ
فاختفي يـا نجـومْ — وانطفئ يا قمر
من سراجي الضئيل — أستمدّ البصر !

باب قلبي حصــينْ — من صنوف الكدرْ
فاهجمي يا همـومْ — في المسـا والسّحر
وازحفي يـا نحوس — بالشّقا والضجر
وانزلي بالألــوفْ — يا خطوب البشـر
باب قلبي حصــينْ — من صنوف الكدر !

وحليفـي القضــاء — ورفيقـي القَـدَرْ
فاقـدحي يا شرورْ — حول قلبي الشّرر
واحفـري يا مَنونْ — حول بيتي الحُفَر
لست أخشى العذابْ — لست أخشى الضرر
وحليفي القضــاء — ورفيقي القَـدَرَ !

And blame not Fate.
Whoever has lost a jewel
Will find it again in the grave.
Go back to the bosom of the earth.

Peace Of Mind

The roof of my house is of steel; its pillars, of stone;
Then blow, O winds! moan, O trees!
Swim, O clouds! fall in torrents of rain!
Roar, O thunder! I fear no danger!
The roof of my house is of steel; its pillars, of stone.

From my dim lamp I seek light to see
Whenever the night grows long and darkness spreads,
And even if the dawn dies, and the day ends its life.
Vanish, O stars! put out your light, O moon!
From my dim lamp, I seek light to see.

The door of my heart is made strong for all kinds of sorrow.
So come forward, O woes, at evening or at twilight!
Advance, O misfortunes with misery and boredom;
Descend in thousands, O mishaps of men!
The door of my heart is made strong for all kinds of sorrow.

Fate is my ally, and destiny is my travelling mate.
So descend with lightnings around my heart, O evils.
Lay siege around my house, O Death!
I fear no torture and I fear no injury!
Fate is my ally; destiny, my travelling mate.

العراك

دخل الشيطانُ قلبي فرأى فيه ملاك ْ
وبلمح الطّرف ما بينهما اشتدّ العراك
ذا يقول : البيت بيتي ! فيعيد القولَ ذاك
وأنا أشهد ما يجري ولا أبـدي حراك

سائلاً ربي : « أفي الأكوان من ْ ربّ سواك
جبلت قلبي من البدء يداه ويـداكَ ؟ »

وإلى اليوم أراني في شكـــوك وارتباك ْ
لستُ أدري أرجيمٌ في فؤادي أم مـــلاك ْ

ايليا أبو ماضي

الطلاسم

جئتُ لا أعلمُ مِن أينَ ولكنّني أتيتُ
ولَقد أبصَرتُ قُدّامي طَريقـاً فَمَشيتُ
وسأبقى مَاشياً إن شئتُ هَذا أم ْ أبَيتُ
كيفَ جئتُ ؟ كيفَ أبصَرتُ طريقي
لستُ أدري !

أجَديدٌ أم قَديمٌ أنا في هَـــذا الوُجودْ
هَل أنا حرٌ طَليقٌ أم ْ أسيرٌ في القيودْ
هَل ْ أنا قائدُ نَفسي في حيَاتي أم مَقُودْ
أتَمَنّى اتّنيَ أدري ولكن ْ
لست أدري !

وطَريقي ، ماطَريقي ؟ أطَويـــلٌ أم قصير
هَل ْ أنا أصعَدُ أم ْ أهبطُ فيه أم ْ أغُورْ

34

The Struggle

The Devil entered my heart, and in it saw an angel.
And in the twinkling of an eye a violent fight broke out
      between them.
One said, "This house is mine!" and the other said it was his,
While I witness what goes on, without the slightest move,
Asking my Lord: "Is there in all creation a god besides You,
Whose hand, together with Yours, fashioned my heart from the
      beginning?"
And until today I see myself in doubt and confusion,
Not knowing whether in my heart is a demon or an angel.

Īlīyā Abū Māḍī

Cryptic Charms

I came—whence, I know not—but I came.
I saw before me a road, so I walked,
And shall continue to walk, whether I will or no—
How did I come? How did I see my road?
I know not.

Am I new, or old, in this existence?
Am I truly free, or a prisoner in chains?
Do I lead myself through my life, or am I led?
I wish to know, and yet—
I know not.

And my road: what is my road? is it long, or short?
Do I climb, or descend, along it, or walk on a level path?

35

أأنا السَّائِرُ في الدَّربِ أمِ الـدَّربُ يَـسِـيرْ
أمْ كِلاَنَـا واقِـفٌ والدَّهرُ يجري ؟
لَستُ أدري !

*

لَيتَ شِعري وأنا في عَالَمِ الغَيبِ الأمينْ
أتُراني كُنتُ أدري أنّني فيه دَفينْ
وبأنّي سَوفَ أبدو وبأنّي سَأكونْ
أمْ تُراني كُنتُ لا أُدركُ شيئاً ؟ ..
لَستُ أدري !

*

اتُراني قَبلَما اصبَحتُ إنساناً سَوِيّاً
أتُراني كُنتُ مَحواً أمْ تُراني كُنتُ شيّاً
ألِهذا اللُّغزِ حَـلٌّ أم سَيَبقى أبـدِيّاً
لَستُ أدري .. ولِمـاذا لستُ أدري ؟ ..
لَستُ أدري !

* *

فوزي المعلوف

ملك في الهواء

في عباب الفضاء فوق غيومه
فوق نسره
ونجمته
حيث بث الهوى بثغر نسيمه
كل عطره
ورقته

موطن الشاعر المحلِّق ــ منذ   البدء لكن بروحه لا بجسمه
انزلته فيه عروس قوافيه   بعيداً عن الوجود وظلمه
ملك قبّة السماء لـه قصـر   وقلب الأثير مسرح حكمه

36

Is it I who travel the road, or the road which travels?
Or do both of us stand still while Time runs on—
I know not.

Would that I had known, while I was in the safe world
        of the unseen:
Did I perceive that I was buried in it?
And that I would appear—that I would be?
Or do you think that I knew nothing?—
I know not.

Do you think that, before I became a created man,
I was a mere void? Or was I something?
Has this mystery a solution, or will it remain eternal?
I know not—and why do I not know?—
I know not!

Fawzī al-Maʿlūf

Canto I: King in the Air

On the lofty heights of heaven above cloud, eagle, and star where
        love scatters on breezes all its perfume and tenderness,
Lies the land of the poet who—in spirit, not body—has soared
        from the first.
His muse placed him there far from the world and its cruelty;
A king, whose palace is the vault of the sky and whose rule ranges
        through the aether's heart;

ضارب في الفضاء موكبه النور   وأتباعـــه عرائس حلمــه –
ملْكه ركنه الهواء ، وما اقواه   ركناً قــام الخلود بدَعمه
عرشه سدّة السحاب عليهــا   نفض الليل كل رهبة رسمه
تاجه ُ هالة ُ يُنضِّد في فضتها   الأفق بدرَه قرب نجمـــه
والدجى طيلسانه فاح كافور   دراريه فــوق عنبر فحمه
والثريا في كفـــه صولجان   درّه ُ لَمَّه الصبــاح بكمه
ملك طائر بغير جناحــين   بأمر الخيــال يقضي وباسمه
يا جناح الخيال اقوى جنـاح   انت يلوي ظهر الرياح لصدمه
ليت شعري ما الشاعر ابن ُ لهذي   الأرض الا بلحمه وبعظمه
فاذا اختـار هجرها برضاه   افما جاءها مقوداً برغمه ْ
هو منها وليس منها ،فما زال   غريباً ما بين ابنــاء أُمـّه

أوراق متناثرة

نجمة الليل ، رحمة ً فضلوعي
من شجوني
تتمزَّق
كفكفي السيل ، انه في دموعي
من عيوني
يتدفَّق

واذكريني بين الكواكب ، وادعي   لي ، عسى يهتدي إلي السلام ُ
عشت بين المنى ، يراود نفسي   خُلَّبٌ من طيوفهــا وعقام
أقتفيها وفي يــديَّ فــؤادي   ثم ألوي وفي يــديَّ حطام
أيّ حــلم سبَكتْه ُ ذهبيـّاً   لم تُذبه ُ بنارهــا الايام

who wanders in space attended by light, followed by the brides
of his dreams.

His kingdom is founded on air, and how mighty that foundation
laid on eternity.

His throne is a seat of clouds, whereon night has shed awesome
designs.

His crown is an aureole of silver, wherein the horizon has set
moon by star.

Dusk cloaks him, its bright stars diffusing essence of camphor
above amber-perfumed night.

The Pleiades in his hand are a scepter whose pearls morning gath-
ers into its sleeves.

He is a king flying without wings, ruling by the power of imagina-
tion and renown:

O wings of imagination, mightiest of wings, against whom the
winds break their back.

Would that I knew if the poet—but for his flesh and bone—be
not a son of this earth,

To leave her if he chose, at will; for was he not led to her un-
willingly?

He is hers, yet not hers, always a stranger among his mother's
sons.

Canto VIII: Strewn Leaves

O evening star, have pity, for my breast is torn with grief;
Hold back the flood! it gushes forth in tears from my eyes.

Remember me among the stars and pray for me; perhaps peace
will find me.

I have lived among yearnings, their visions seducing my soul with
barren delusions.

I pursue them, my heart in my hands; I turn, and in my hands are
fragments.

What dream have I cast of gold that the fire of passing days did
not melt?

ورجاء حبكته ، من خيوط   النور ، لم ينسدل عليه ظلام

اي عود حملتـــه للتلهـي   لم تقطّعِ اوتاره الآلام

ونشيد ٌ وقّعْتـــه للتأسي   لم يعكّـره ُ بالأنين الغـرام

اي كأسٍ قرّبته من شفاهـي   لم تَحُل حنظلاً عليه المدام

وفؤاد ذوّبتُ فيه فؤادي   لم يضِع عنده لعهدي ذمام

اي طيف عانقته في منامي   لم يكلّلـه دمع عيني السِجام

وهناء زرعته في ضلوعـي   لم يكن منــه للذبول طعام

ليت شِعري ، والليل يعقبـه   الفجر، متى يعقب البكاءَ ابتسام

ضاع عمري، سعياً وراء رَسوم   خططتها في الشاطىء الأقدام

عشت ابني على الرمال ، وهَل يثبت ركنٌ ، له الرمال دعام

خليل مطران

وردة ماتت

ما الذي تبغين من جوبك يا   شبهات الطير ؟ قالت وابانت

«نحن آمال الصبى ــ كانت لنا   ههنا محبوبة عاشت وعانت

كانت الوردة في جنتنـــا   ملكت بالحق ، والجنة دانت

ما لبثنا ان رايناهــا وقـد   هبطت عن ذلك العرش وبانت

فترانـا نتحرّى ابـــداً   اثرها او نتلاقى حيث كانت»

Or hope woven from threads of light on which dark did not fall?

What lute have I borne for pleasure whose strings pain has not
snapped?

Or song have I played for solace not muddied by love's lament?

What cup have I raised to my lips whose wine has not bittered to
colocynth?

Or heart in which I have melted mine that has not betrayed my
trust?

What vision have I held in sleep that has not left, wreathed in my
flowering tears?

Or joy planted within my breast that was not eaten by decay?

Would that I knew—dawn following night—when a smile will
follow tears.

My life was squandered pursuing traces left by feet upon the
shore.

I have lived, building upon sand; and what founded on sand can
endure?

Khalīl Muṭrān

A Rose that Died

O questing birds, what seek you in your wanderings?
        They made answer:
We are the hopes of youth; and here our beloved
        lived and suffered.
She was the rose in our garden, reigning
        justly with the submission of all therein.
Yet all too soon we saw her fall from her throne,
        then disappear.
And so you see us ever searching for some trace of her,
        or flocking where once she was wont to be.

نيرون

ذلك الشعب الذي آتاه نصرا   هو بالسبة من نيرون احرى

اي شيء كان نيرون الذي عبدوه؟   كان فظ الطبع غــرّا

قزمة هم نصبوه عاليـــاً   وجثوا بين يديه فاشمخرا

ضخَّموه واطالـوا فيئـه   فترامى يملا الآفـاق فجرا

منحــوه مـن قواهم ما به صـار طاغوتـا واضـرّا

انما يبطش ذو الامر اذا لــم يَخف بطش الأولى ولَّوه أمرا

من يلم نيرون اني لائــم   امة لو كهرته ارتدَّ كَهْرا

كلُّ قوم خالقو « نيرونهم »   «قيصر» قيل له ام قيل «كسْرى»

الياس أبو شبكة

شهوة الموت

نَاقِمٌ عَلَى السَّمَا   حَاقِدٌ عَلَى البَشَرْ

سَاخِطٌ عَلَى القَضَا   ثَائِرٌ عَلَى القَدَرْ

غَيْرَ قَطْرَة المَسَا   لاَ أُحِبُّ في السَّحَرْ

صِرْتُ أَمْقُتُ الصَّفَا   صِرْتُ أَعْشَقُ الكَدَرْ

غَيْرَ مَشْهَد الدِّمَا   لاَ أُحِبُّ في الصُّوَرْ

نَاقِمٌ عَلَى السَّمَا   والبَشَرْ

42

Nero

That people which bestowed victory upon Nero
    is more deserving of shame than he.
What was that Nero whom they worshipped?
    He was coarse and ignorant,
A dwarf whom they raised on high.
    They crawled before him and he grew in arrogance.
They glorified him and extended his shadow
    until it filled the earth with crime.
They gave him of their power, so he
    became a tyrant over them, and worse.
The ruler oppresses only when he has no fear
    of the ruled revolting.
Some denounce Nero, but I, the nation;
    had it defied him, retreat would have been his lot.
Every nation creates its own Nero,
    be he called "Caesar" or "Chosroes."

Ilyās Abū Shabakah

Lust For Death

Rebelling against Heaven,
Detesting mankind
    Of fate resentful
    By destiny enraged
Except for the dew of night
I love nothing of the dawn.
    I've grown to loathe happiness;
    I've fallen in love with gloom.
Of what I see I love nothing
Except the sight of blood,
    Rebelling against Heaven
    And mankind.

جَمِّلِي لِيَ ٱلجَسَدْ   وَٱسْكُبِي لِيَ الرَّحيقْ

لاَ تُفَكِّري بِغَــدْ   قَدْ يَجِي وَلاَ نُفيقْ

مَا لَنَا وَلْلأَبَــدْ   إِنَّ سِــرَّهُ عَميقْ

الْهَوَى إِذَا أتّقَــدْ   كَان لِلْبِلَى طَريــقْ

فَلْنَمُتْ يَــداً بِيَدْ   وَلْنُغَيِّبْ البَريــقْ

بَيْنَ شَهْوَةِ الْجَسَدْ   وَالرَّحيقْ

ألبير أديب

وفـاء

لمْ أُحْبِبْكِ يوماً
بل احببتُ فيكِ نَفسي
وانعكاسات رؤَايَ الحالِمةَ
واعرُف انّنِي في خاطرِكِ
لم أَكن غير انتقامٍ
لحبّ اضعتهْ
عشنا معاً
فتألّفتْ مِنا اسطورةٌ كاذبةٌ
غُصَّتْ بها رُوحانا الظَّماَّ
وعرفَتْنا الدُنيا انشودةً خالدةً
فيَا لهَوان الهَوى
لست لي ولَم اكُنْ لكِ
سأذهَبُ وتذهبين
غريبَيْنِ عاشَا معاً
وأبقيَا من بعدِهما
... اكذوبهْ ...

44

Adorn for me your body
And fill my cup with wine.
> Do not think of tomorrow;
> It may come when we no longer wake.
What do we care for eternity?
Its secrets are hidden deep.
> Love, once ablaze,
> Is the way to death.
Let us then die, hand in hand,
And bury the light of life,
> Amid lust
> And wine.

Albert Adib

Fidelity

I never loved you
But loved myself in you
The reflections of a dream, a vision
And I know that in your mind
I was only the revenge
For some wasted love
We lived together
And from us was composed a lying legend
That stifled our souls in pain
While the world thought us some eternal song
O the contempt of love
You were not mine, I was not yours
I shall leave, you will leave
Two strangers that lived together
Leaving behind them
Lies

سعيد عقل

سمراء

سمراءُ ، يا حُلمَ الطُفولَة ،
وتَمنّعَ الشفَــةِ البَخيلَـة .
لا تقربـي منّـي ، وظلّـي
فكـرةً ، لِغَدي ، جميلَة .

*

قلبي مليءٌ بالفُراغِ
الحُلْوِ ، فاجتني دخولَــه .
أخشى عليه يَغَصّ
بالقُبَل المطيّبَة البَليلَة .
٥ ويغيب في الآفاق ،
عبرَ الهُدب من عينٍ كحيلة ! ...

*

ما آخذٌ منك البهاءُ
ومن غَدائرك الجديلَــه ؟
ضوءاً ؟ فدَيتُ الضوءَ يولــدَ
طَيّ لفتتك العليلَــهْ ؛
ويقول للبَسَمَات ثغرُك :
« لَوّني زَهْـــرَ الحميلَــهْ » ؛
فالأرضُ بعدك يَقظةٌ
من هجعــة الحُلم الثقيلَـهْ ،
١٠ طَربتْ ، كأنّ سَنى ابتسامِك
كوّةُ الأمل الضّئيلَهْ .

*

سمراء ، ظَلّـي لــذّةً
بين اللذائــذ مُستحيلَهْ ؛

46

Sa'id 'Aql

Samra

Samra, o childhood dream,
Impregnable, miserly lips,
Approach me not, remain as
A thought of beauty for my morrow.
My heart is full of a sweet
Void; so enter it not.
I fear it would choke
Beneath your moist, perfumed kisses,
And vanish over the horizon
Through your kohl-anointed lashes.
What has beauty taken
From you and your plaited trees?
Its light? I would gladly die for the light
Born of your languid glance.
Your mouth replies to a smile:
"Go, paint the copse's flowers."
The earth as you pass is an awakening
From the deep slumber of dream,
Joyous as if your flashing smile
Were some small chink of hope.
Samra, remain one among
The unattainable delights;

ظَلِّي على شفَتيّ شوقَهما ،
وفي جَفنــي ذهولَــهْ ؛
ظَلِّي الغدَ المنشودَ
يسبقُنا الممات إليه غِيلَــهْ .

قصر الحبيبة

أبتَني ، كلّ ليلــة ،
لك قصــراً منــوّراً ،
حَجَراً من زُمــرّدٍ ،
ومن الماس أحْجُـــرا .
أيّ لون ؟ سماءُ عينيك
أم خُضَّرةُ الــذُرى ؟
انا قصري من كــلِّ مـا
شئت : كونــي فيحضُرا .
٥   طيّعٌ ، واهزجــي يَطِــرْ
بك طيراً ، ويَسكَرا .
خَيْطُ ضوءٍ يَرقى بــه
صَوْبَ نجمـَـين غَــوّرا ،
وثـــوانٍ يدفعنَـــه ،
غُمِّض الجَفن سُمَّرا .

*

واذا جُزتُما المـدى ،
ومن النـــور أبحُــرا ،
أنا ، إن أنت همت بــي ،
والسُهى حولنــا يُــرى ،
أبتني في النجوم لــي
بعلبكّــا ، وتَدْمُــرا !
بالغيّ قُبّــة بهـا
يُصنعُ الحُلَــمُ والكَرى ،

The object of my lip's desire
And of my distraught gaze;
That morrow for which we long
And death, stealing forward, grasps.

The Palace of My Beloved

I will build for you each night
A palace luminous
With whole blocks of emerald
And diamond stones.
Shall it be skyblue as your eyes,
Or green as the hilltops?
It will be made of your wishes:
Be, and the palace too shall be.
Sing softly, and obedient it will take **you**
And fly aloft like a drunken bird,
And rise on a thread of light,
Seeking two sunken stars;
Driven on by the seconds of time,
Their eyes closed in the discourse of night.

When together you have traversed
The expanse, and the oceans of light,
And reached the dome of heaven
Where sleep and dreams are made,

١٠ فاسألي عــن أصابـــع
لِيَ ، مسَّتْ ذاك الثَّرى ،
زرعتْهُ ، ورحَّبَـــتْ
قبل أن زرت – أزْهُـــرا ،
علَّـــه يغتدي إلى
قصرك الحلو ، مَعْبَـــرا !

*

وإذا ما مَلَلْتـــه ،
واسى وحشـــة عَـــرى ،
وتذكَّرت أرضَنَـــا
ورُباها ، وَالأَنْهُـــــرا ،
١٥ فاهجسي بي أُقبِلْ ، وفي
بُردتي الكـــونُ أخضرا .
طبتِ ، يا مَطلبي ، اطلبي ،
بَعد هدمٍ ، فأعمُـــرا .
واقول : « امرحي ، امرحـي ،
واقطفي الشُّهبَ كالكُرى .
٢٠ لكِ ، للَّهو ، للهـــوى ،
بُدِّلَ الكـــونُ منظرا » .

صلاح لبكي

موت الورود

اذ يموت الوردُ لا يَمَّحي   الا السنا واللونُ والرونقُ
ويخلدُ الطيبُ فإمّا جرَتْ   ريحُ الصبا من جانبٍ يعبقُ
الوردُ لا يفنى فناءً ولـو   ماتَ وألوى عودُه المورقُ

50

Ask after those my fingers
Which once touched that soil,
Sowed there flowers of welcome
Before your visit came,
That might one day mark
The way to your fine palace.

Should you tire of the palace,
Of the pain of solitude and grief,
And remember this our earth,
Its hills and streams,
Then whisper and I shall come,
The world's verdure in my cloak.
With sickness past, ask, O my desire,
That I erect anew the ruin.
If you love with a passion
That sheds luster on the dimmest star,
Then will I build myself in the skies
A Baalbek or Palmyra,
And say: "Rejoice, be gay,
Catch each comet like a ball,"
With the world as but a show
For you, your amusement and your whim.

Ṣalāḥ Labakī

The Death of Roses

When roses die,
Only the brilliance, the color, the beauty vanish.
The scent abides
Lingering with the flowing of the eastern wind.
Roses do not perish,
Even if the leafy stem bow its head and die.

الليل

رحِمَ الليلُ أَعـــينَ السهّاد — ومَحَتْ كفُّــه الشعاعَ المنادي

أخرَسَتْ كلَّ صيحةٍ في فمِ الشمسِ — ومالَتْ بكبريـــاءَ المهاد

أيُّ ربٍّ يا ليلُ انتَ رئيـــف — بتجنّي الورى ورجسِ العباد

بسمةٌ أنْتَ في السفوحِ وعفـــوٌّ — دائمُ الفيضِ دائمُ الميـــلاد

كلُّ حسنٍ من فضلِ كفّيك حسنٌ — روعة الصمتِ والجلالِ البادي

ميلاد الشاعر

وَحْدي أَنا يَا رَبِّ وَحْدي نَشْوانَ [1] مِنْ سَأَمٍ وَزُهْدِ

وَحْدي كأَنَّ الشَّمْسَ لَمْ تَطْلَعْ عَلَى الدُّنْيَا بِوَعْدِ

وَحْدي وَلَوْ أَنَّ الرَّبيعَ مُصَفِّقٌ والنُّورُ يَهْدي

وَمَطَارِحُ الآفاقِ أنْغامٌ تَلُوحُ لي بِرَغْدِ

والوَرْدُ مِنْ حَوْلي مَدَى الآفاقِ يَخْفُقُ فَوْقَ وَرْدِ

أَنا والشِّتَاءَ أَسُومُهُ [2] ويَسُومُني بَرْدٌ بِبَرْدِ

وَحْدي فَمَا الإِنْسَانُ لِي بِأَخٍ ولا هُوَ لِي بِجَدِّ

أَنا لَسْتُ مِنْ هذا التُّرَابِ وَلَسْتُ مِنْ حَسَدٍ وَحِقْدِ

فَلَقَدْ تَرَكْتُ وَعِشْتُ في مَلإٍ [3] مِنَ الأَحْلاَمِ فَرْدِ

وَقَطَعْتُ مَا بَيْني وَبَيْـــنَ الأَرْضِ مِنْ صِلَةٍ وَوُدِّ

يوسف الخال

العمر

نُزيحُ موجةَ الصقيعِ عن وجوهِنا

نحكي لها حكايةَ الربيعِ :

كيف يبسمُ الهواءُ ،

تُنشدُ الطيورُ ، كيف

يرقصُ الشجرْ

52

The Night

The night has compassion for the sleepless eye.
Its hand strikes out the herald ray.
It smothers every cry in the mouth of the sun
And robs lofty hills of haughtiness.
What a god you are, night.
Merciful toward the lowly acts of mortals,
Toward the shameful acts of men.
A smile among the heights you are;
Forgiveness with an everflowing source.
All beauty in your hand's gift:
The awesome silence, the sublime grandeur.

Birth of the Poet

Alone, o Lord, alone, drunk on boredom and disgust;
Alone, as if the sun had not risen over the world with its promise;
Alone, though the spring claps its hands in joy and the light glows
forth,
And the spacious horizons are melodies that gaily shine,
Horizons all around decked with pulsating, heaped-up roses;
Alone with winter, visiting cold pain on each other;
Alone, with no man for father or brother.
I belong not to this soil, nor to envy and rancour;
I have left all behind, living alone in a fullness of dreams,
And served all kinship and love between me and the earth.

Yūsuf al-Khāl

Old Age

We wipe the chill wave from our faces
And tell ourselves the story of spring:
How the breeze smiles,
The birds sing,
The trees dance;

وكيف تفتح النّواة في الثّرى
عروقها ويُعقَدُ الثمر .

نحكي لها حكاية الخريفِ
حين تنحني الظلالُ ،
والمساء يستطيل ثم بغتةً
تلوح نجمة أو يسطع القمرْ ،
وحين يسقط السياجِ ، حينما
تنبسط الحقول نظرةً عاريةً
على مدى البصرْ .

نحكي لها
حكايةَ الصيف الذي يجيئنا
على جناحَي نغمة دافئة
أو قفزة من جندبٍ سعيدْ ،
ونحن نجمّع الغلالَ تارةً
وتارةً نعيدْ
ذكرى وقوف غيمةٍ هنا ،
هناك في البعيدْ .

نَزيّحها
نحكي لها حكاية الفصول كلِّها
لكنها
تغور في عروقنا ، تضيعْ
نظنّها تضيعْ
وهي التي تلوحُ فجأةً
في شعرةٍ تبيضٌ ههنا
أو شفةٍ تجوعْ .

54

How the seed stretches its roots in the soil
And bears fruit.

We tell ourselves the story of autumn,
When the shadows are bowed
And evening lengthens,
Then suddenly a star appears,
Or a moon shines,
And when the fence falls,
The fields stretch out naked,
As far as the eye can see.

We tell ourselves the story of summer,
Which comes to us on the wings
Of a warm melody,
Or the leap of a joyous swallow,
While we gather the crop,
Or recall the halt of a cloud,
Here and there in the distance.

We wipe the chill wave from our faces
And tell ourselves the seasons' story.
But the wave sinks deep in our veins and vanishes.
We think it vanishes,
Yet, suddenly, it appears—
Here, in a hair turned white,
There, in a lip turned dry.

السفر

وفي النهار نهبط المرافىءَ الأمانَ
والمراكبَ الناشرة الشراع للسَّفَرْ .
نهتف يا ، يا بحرنا الحبيب ، يا القريبُ
كالجفون من عيوننا
نجيء وحدنا ؛
رفاقنا وراء تلكمُ الجبال آثروا
البقاء في سُباتهم ونحن نؤثر السفرْ .
أخبرنا الرعاة ههنا
عن جزُر هناك تعشق الخطرْ
وتكره القَعود والحَذَرْ ،
عن جزر تصارع القدَرْ
وتزرع الأضراس في القفار
مُدُناً ، حروفَ نور تكتبُ السِيَرْ
وتملأ العيون بالنظرْ .
بها ، بمثل لونها العجيب يحلمُ
الكبار في الصغَرْ .
إذَّاك نصعد المراكبَ الحاملةَ
الزجاجَ والصنوبرَ ، الحاملة الحريزَ
والخمورَ من بلادنا ، الحاملةَ الثمرْ .
نصيحُ يا مراكبُ !
يا سلّماً يرقى بنا ،
يصلنا بغيرنا ،
يأتي لنا بما غلا ،
يأخذ منا ما حلا ...

يا انت ما مراكب ،
جئنا إلَيك وحدنا ،
رفاقنا الهناكَ في الرمال آثروا البقاءَ
تحتَ رحمة الهجير والنقيق والضجَرْ

The Voyage

At daybreak we descend to our sheltered harbors
And the ships with their sails unfurled depart.
We call out: o beloved sea,
Close to us as these eyelids to our eyes!
We come alone, choosing to venture forth,
While our comrades, behind those mountains, choose to
    slumber on.

Our shepherds have told us
Of islands in love with danger
And hating sloth and caution;
Of islands wrestling with fate,
Planting, with tooth and nail,
Cities in the desert,
And letters of light encoding histories
To fill men's eyes with wonder.
Of them, and their magic color, the great dream while young.

Then we embark on the ships,
Laden with glass and pinewood,
With silk and fruit and wines.
We call out: o ships!
O upward-bearing ladder!
Linking us with the world beyond,
Bringing us precious treasure
And bearing our finery in return!
O ships!
We have come to you alone.
Our comrades, there in the desert, chose to remain
At the mercy of heat and croaking boredom,

ونحن نؤثر السفرْ ،
أخبرنا الرعاة في جبالنا
عن جزرٍ يغمرها المطرْ ،
يغمرها الغمام والخزام والمطرْ ،
عن جزرٍ لا تعرف الضجرْ .
بها ، بمثلِ لونها الغريبِ يحلمُ
الكبارُ في الصغَرْ .

وقبلما نهمُّ بالرحيل نذبح الخرافَ
واحداً لعشتروت ، واحداً لأدونيسَ ،
واحداً لبعلَ ، ثم نرفع المراسيَ الحديدَ
من قرارة البَحَرْ ،
ونبدأ السفرْ :
هلّــــلويا .
هلّــــلويا .
وفي هنيهة تغيب عن عيوننا
الجبال ، والمرافىءُ الأمانُ ، والمرابعُ
المليئةُ اليدينِ بالزهَرْ :
هلّــــلويا .
هلّــــلويا .
هلّــــلويا .
ونبدأ السفرْ
وسيرةَ الرجوع والصراع والظفَرْ .

While we choose to voyage.
Our mountain shepherds have told us
Of islands drenched in rain,
Drenched in clouds, in lavender and rain,
Of islands that know no boredom.
Of them, and their magic color, the great dream while young.

Before we set sail we slaughter sheep,
One for Astarte, one for Adonis
And one for Baal.
Then from the seabed
We haul in the iron anchor
And begin our voyage.
Halleluja!
Halleluja!
An instant, and there vanish from our sight
The mountains,
The sheltered meadows,
The land brimming over with flowers.
Halleluja!
Halleluja!
Halleluja!
We begin our voyage
And the tale of struggle, of triumph and homecoming.

خليل حاوى

البحار والدرويش

طوّف مع « يوليس » في المجهول ، ومع « فاوست »
ضحّى بروحه ليفتدي المعرفة ، ثم انتهى إلى اليأس من
العلم في هذا العصر ، تنكّر له مع « هكسلي » فأبحر إلى
ضفاف « الكنج » ، منبت التصوف ... !
لم ير غير طين ميت هنا ، وطين حار هناك .
طين بطين ! !

بعدَ أنْ عانَى دُوارَ البَحرِ ،
والضَوْءَ المداجي عَبْرَ عَتَمات الطريقْ ،
ومَدى المجهول يَنْشَقُّ عن المَجهولِ ،
عن مَوت مَحيقْ
ينْشرُ الأكفانَ زُرْقاً للغريقْ ،
وتمطّت في فراغِ الأفقِ أشداقُ كهوفٍ
لفّها وهجُ الحَريقْ ،
بعد أنْ راوَغهُ الريحُ
رماهُ الريحُ للشرْقِ العَريقْ .

حطَّ في أرْضٍ حكى عَنها الرُّواةْ :
حانةٌ كَسْلى ، أساطيرْ ، صلاةْ
ونَخيلٌ فاترُ الظلِّ رخيُّ الهَيْنَماتْ
مَطْرَحٌ رَطْبٌ يُميت الحِسَّ
في أعْصابه الحَرّى ، يميت الذكريَاتْ ،
والصدى النائي المدوّي
وغوَايات المواني النائياتْ .
آه لو يسعفُهُ زُهْدُ الدَراويشِ العُراةْ
دوَّختهُم « حَلَقاتُ الذكْرِ »
فاجْتازُوا الحَيَاةْ .
حَلَقاتٌ حلَقاتْ

60

Khalil Hāwī

The Mariner and The Dervish

He wandered with Ulysses in the unknown and with Faust he sacrificed his soul for the sake of knowledge. Then finally, in our present age, he despaired of science and, estranged like Huxley, set sail for the banks of the Congo, that fountainhead of Sufism. Here, he saw naught but lifeless clay; there, naught but warm clay. Clay exchanged for clay!

After bearing with seasickness,
The false light across the darkened path,
And unknown expanses unfolding out of the unknown,
Out of death, encompassing,
Spreading blue shrouds for the drowned,
Unfolding cavernous jaws on the horizon's void
Wrapped in the fire's blaze;
Then, tricked by the wind,
He was cast up on the shores of the antique East.

He put down in a land storytellers speak of,
A slothful tavern, legends, prayer,
The feeble shade of listlessly murmuring palm trees,
A humid backwash that numbs all feeling
In heated nerves, numbs all memory,
The distant repeated echo
And the lure of distant ports.
O if the naked, ascetic dervishes would but help him!
Giddied by their "circles of remembrance" they had crossed
The frontier of life.
Circles, circles

حَوْلَ درويشٍ عتيق ْ
شرَّشَت رجلاهُ في الوَحْلِ وبات ْ
ساكناً ، يَمتصُّ ما تَنضَحُهُ الأرْضُ المَوات ،
في مطاوي جلده ِ يَنْمو طُفَيلِيُّ النبات ْ :
طحلبٌ شاخَ على الدَّهرِ وَلَبْلابٌ صفيق ْ .
غائبٌ عن حسِّهِ لَنْ يَسْتَفيق ْ .
حَظُّهُ مِنْ مَوْسِمِ الخِصْبِ المدوِّي
في العُروق ْ
رُقَعٌ تَزْرَعُ بالزهو الأنيق ْ
جلدَهْ الرثَّ العتيق ْ

— هات خبِّرْ عن كنوزٍ سمَّرت ْ
عينَيك في الغَيْبِ العَميق ْ

— قابعٌ في مَطرَحَي من ألف ألفٍ
قابعٌ في ضفّة « الكَنجِ » العَريق ْ
طُرُقاتُ الأرْضِ مهما تتناءَى
عند باني تَنْتَهي كلُّ طريق ْ ،
وبكوخي يستَريحُ التَوْأمانِ :
اللهُ ، والدهرُ السَحيق ..
... وَأَرى ، ماذا أرى ؟
مَوتاً ، رَماداً وَحَريق ْ ... !
نَزَلَتْ في الشاطىء الغَرْبِيِّ
حدِّقْ تَرَهَا ... أمْ لا تُطيق ْ ؟
... ذَلكَ الغولَ الذي يُرْغي
فيُرغي الطينُ محموماً ، وتنْحَمُّ المَواني
وَإذا بالأرْضِ حُبْلى تَتَلَوَّى وتُعاني
فَوْرَةً في الطينِ من آنٍ لآن .
فَوْرَةً كانت أثينا ثُمَّ رُوماً ... !
وهجَ حمّى حشرجتْ في صَدرِ فاني

62

Around an antique dervish,
His legs rooted in the mud, motionless
He stands, absorbs the distillations of barren earth,
And in the folds of his skin sprout parasitic plants,
Watermoss aged by the passage of time and ivy thickly growing.
Untouched by feeling he will never wake,
His share of the season of fertility that courses through
         the veins
Only a cloth that plants elegant beauty
On his ancient tattered skin.

—Come, tell of the treasures that have driven
Your eyes down into the deep unknown.
—Crouching in this backwash a thousand times a thousand years,
Crouching on the primeval Congo's bank,
The roads of the world, however distant,
At my door all end, all,
And in my hut rest the twins:
God and boundless time.
And I see . . . what?
Death, ashes and fire,
Descending on the western shore!
Gaze out, you will see!
Or can you not bear that foaming ghoul?
The clay too foams in fever,
The ports are stricken with fever,
And behold, the earth is pregnant, writhes and suffers,
And now and then bursts forth,
Bursts forth with an Athens or Rome!
As the heat of a fever rattling in a wasted chest

خلّفتْ مَطرَحَهَا بعضَ بُثُورٍ ،
ورمادٍ مِن نُفايات الزمانِ

ذَلكَ الغُولُ المُعاني
ما أراهُ غيرَ طفلٍ
مِن مواليد الثواني
وَيَداً شمطاءَ مِنْ أعصابه تَنسُلُ
أكفاناً لهُ ، والمَوْتُ دانِي
وتَرَاني
قابعاً في مَطرَحي من ألف ألفٍ
قابعاً في ضفّة « الكنج » العَريقْ
وبكوخي يستريحُ التَوأمانِ :
اللهُ والدهرُ السحيق

أتُرَى حُمِّلتَ مِن صدقِ الرؤى
ما لا تطيقْ ؟
ـ خلِّني ! ماتت بعَيْنيَّ
منارات الطَريقْ
خلِّني أمضِ إلى ما لستُ أدري
لن تغاويني المَواني النائياتْ
بعضُها طينٌ محمّى
بعضُها طينٌ مواتْ
آهَ كم أُحرقْتُ في الطين المحمّى
آهَ كم متُّ مع الطين المَواتْ
لن تغاويني المَواني النائياتْ ،
خلِّني للبحر ، للرّيح ، لموت
ينشُرُ الأكفانَ زُرقاً للغَريقْ ،
مُبْحِرٌ ماتَتْ بعَينيه منارات الطريقْ
ماتَ ذَاكَ الضوءُ في عينيه ماتْ
لا البطولاتُ تنجِّيه ، ولا ذلُّ الصلاةْ .

64

Leaves behind an odd blister
And ashes from the refuse of time.

That suffering ghoul,
I see him only as a child born of the seconds' passage,
And a gray-haired hand unravels from his nerves
His shrouds, and death is near.
And you see me,
Crouching in this backwash a thousand times a thousand years,
Crouching on the Congo's primeval bank,
And in my hut rest the twins:
God and boundless time.
—Do you think yourself burdened with a vision of truth
        unbearable?
—Let me be! the lighthouses on my path are dead to my eye.
Let me walk on to the unknown,
The distant ports will not deceive me,
Some of fevered clay,
Some of lifeless clay.
O how often did I burn in that fevered clay!
O how often did I die in that lifeless clay!
The distant ports will not deceive me:
Leave me to the sea, to the wind, to death
Who spreads blue shrouds for the drowned,
A mariner, to whose eye are dead the lighthouses on the path.
Dead is that light in his eyes, dead;
Heroic deeds save him not, nor humility of prayer.

الجسر

وكَفاني أنَّ لي أطفالَ أترابي
وليَ في حبِّهم خمرٌ وزادْ
مـن حصادِ الحَقلِ عندي ما كفاني
وكَفاني أنَّ لي عيدَ الحصادْ ،
أنَّ لي عيداً وعيدْ
كلّما ضَوَّأ في القَريةِ مصباحٌ جديدْ ،
غيَرَ أنّي ما حملتُ الحبَ للموتى
طيوباً ، ذهباً ، خمراً ، كنوزْ
طفلُهُم يُولدُ خفّاشاً عجوزْ
أين َمَنْ يُفني ويُحيي ويُعيدْ
يتولّى خَلْقَه طفلاً جديدْ
غَسْلهُ بالزيتِ والكبريتِ
مـن نَتَنِ الصديدْ
أيـنَ مَنِ يُفني ويُحيي ويُعيد
يتَولى خَلْقَ فرخِ النسرِ
مِن نَسلِ العَبيدْ

أنكَرَ الطفلُ أباهُ ، أمَّه
ليسَ فيه منهُما شبْهٌ بَعيدْ

ما لهُ يَنْشَقُ فينا البَيتُ بَيتَين
ويَجري البَحرُ ما بَيْنَ جديدٍ وعتيقْ
صرخةٌ ، تقطيعُ أرحامٍ ،
وتَمزيقُ عُروقْ ،
كَيفَ نَبقى تحتَ سَقْفٍ واحدِ
وبِحارٌ بينا .. سورٌ ..
وصَحراءُ رمادٍ باردِ
وجليدْ .
ومتى نظفرُ مِن قبوٍ وسجْنِ

66

The Bridge

Sufficient unto me are the children of my peers,
For in their love I have proviant and wine.
Sufficient unto me is the harvest of the fields,
And the harvest festival,
A festival recurring
Whenever a new lamp is lit in the village.
Not to the dead do I offer my love,
With its perfume and gold, its treasure and wine,
For their offspring is born as an aged bat.
Where is he who will destroy, who will revive and renew?
Who will make that child anew,
Wash him in oil and surphur,
In stinking pus?
Where is he who will destroy, who will revive and renew?
Who will create a young eagle from the offspring of slaves?

The child, showing no trace of its parentage,
Has repudiated both father and mother.

Why is it that our house is split in two?
And that the sea flows between the old and new?
A cry, the shattering of wombs,
The tearing apart of veils.
How can we remain beneath a single roof?
When there are seas between us, and walls,
Deserts of cold ash,
And ice?
When are we to break out of the pit and prison?

ومتى ، ربّاهُ ، نشتدُّ ونبني
بِيَدَينا بَيتنا الحُرَّ الجَديدْ

يَعبرونَ الجسرَ في الصبحِ خفافاً
أضلُعي امتَدَّتْ لَهُم جِسراً وطيدْ
مِن كُهوفِ الشَرقِ ، مِن مُستنقعِ الشَرقِ
إلى الشَرقِ الجديدْ
أضلُعي امتَدَّتْ لَهُم جسراً وطيدْ
« سوفَ يَمضونَ وَتبقى »
« صَنَماً خلّفَهُ الكهّانُ للريح »
« التي تُوسعُهُ جَلْداً وَحرْقاً »
« فارغَ الكَفَّيْنِ ، مصلوباً ، وحيدْ »
« في ليالي الثَلْجِ والأفقُ رمادْ »
« ورمادُ النار ، والخبز رمادْ »
« جامدَ الدَمْعَة في لَيْلِ السهادْ »
« ويُوَافيك مع الصبحِ البريدْ : »
« صَفحَةُ الأخبارِ .. كم تجترُّ ما فيها »
« تُفَلِّيها .. تُعيدْ .. ! »
« سوفَ يَمضونَ وتبقى »
« فارغَ الكَفَّيْنِ ، مصلوباً ، وحيدْ . »

إخرسي يا بُومةً تقرعُ صُدري
بومةُ التاريخِ مني ما تُريدْ ؟
في صَناديقي كُنوزٌ لا تَبيدْ :
فرحي في كُلِّ ما أطعَمتُ
مِن جَوهرِ عُمْري ،
فَرَحُ الأيدي التي أعْطَتْ وإيمانٌ وذِكرى ،
إنَّ لي جَمْراً وخمْراً
إنَّ لي أطفالَ أترابي

68

And when, o Lord, are we to be strong and build with our own
     hands
Our new, free house?
They cross the bridge at dawn, light-footed,
My ribs laid out before them, a solid bridge.
They cross from the caverns and swamps of the old east
Into the new,
My ribs laid out before them a solid bridge.

They will pass on while you remain,
An idol left by the soothsayers for the wind
To lash and burn,
An idol empty-handed, crucified in solitude,
In snowy nights with ashen horizons,
In fiery ashes with bread of ash,
An idol with frozen tears in sleepless nights,
Greeted by the morning with the daily news,
Pored over and consumed.
They will pass on while you remain,
Empty-handed, crucified in solitude.

O owl pecking at my breast, be still.
What does the owl of history want of me?
In my chests there are treasures that never perish.
My joy in the sustenance I gave
Out of the very core of my life
Is the joy of hands that give,
Is a faith and a recollection.
I have wine and a burning coal,
I have the children of my peers,

ولي في حُبِّهم خَمْرٌ وزادْ
مِن حصاد الحَقْلِ عندي ما كفاني
وكَفاني أنَّ لي عيدَ الحصادْ ،
يا مَعادَ الثلج لَن أخْشاكَ
لي خَمْرٌ وجَمْرٌ للمَعادْ

أنسي الحاج

حوار

قولي : بماذا تفكرين ؟
أفكِّر في شمسكَ التي لا تنيرني يا عاشقي .
قولي : بماذا تفكرين ؟
أفكر فيك ، كيف تستطيع ان تصبر على برودة قلبي .
قولي : بماذا تفكرين ؟
أفكر يا عاشقي في جبروتك ، كيف انك تحبني ولا أحبك .

قل : بماذا تفكر ؟
افكر كيف كنت ، وأحزن من اجلك يا حبيبتي .
افكر في شمسي التي اذابتك ، وفي جَلَدي الذي خضّعك ، افكر
في حبي الذي ركّعك ، ثم مَلَّك يا حبيبتي .
أفكر في المرائي يا حبيبتي .
أفكر في القتل .

70

And in their love I have proviant and wine.
Sufficient unto me is the harvest of the fields,
And the harvest festival.
I shall not fear you, o returning snows,
For when you come,
I shall have wine and a burning coal.

Unsī al-Ḥājj

Dialogue

I said:
Tell me, of what are you thinking?
—Of your sun which does not illuminate me, o beloved.
I said:
Tell me, of what are you thinking?
—Of you, and how you can endure the coldness of my heart.
I said:
Tell me, of what are you thinking?
—Of your might, o beloved, of how you can love me, when
I do not love you.

She said:
Tell me, of what are you thinking?
—Of how you once were, and I grieve for you, o beloved.
I think too of my sun which melted you,
Of my patience which made you submit,
Of my love which brought you to your knees,
And then spurned you,
O beloved.
I think of elegies,
O beloved,
I think of murder.

الكاس

لن أتوقّف
لن أتوقف
تحت القَمَر بالثوب الأبيض
غَرَقاً
في اليوم التالي
بين ضَرَبات الصدر

أنت
في قَبّة الضباب
وآبار الكنائس المستطيلة
في الأعياد
وشعشعة الواجهات
وحقول الايقاعات الشعبيّة
ونحل الضجيج اليائس
وإقلاع السفن والحمور
تتبقين لي دون أن أشعر
تتبقين لي وأنا أشعر
فتقفف التجاعيد والطراوات
والأرض تمدّ رأسها
تتبعنا من كلمة إلى كلمة
من عصفور
إلى عصفور

سمعتُ وأنا بعيد
وعندما حاولتُ أن اقرّب
وضعت يدك .
سمعتُ وَأنا بَعيد
ورأيتُ خلف الغابات
الشعوب القديمة .

72

The Cup

I shall not stop,
I shall not stop
Beneath the moon clothed in white,
Drowning in the morrow
With a fast-beating heart.

You remain mine, when I am aware,
You remain mine, when I am unaware.
There, in the dome of mist,
In the wells of spacious churches,
In festivals
And the glimmering of windows,
The fields of folksong,
The desperate hum of din,
The departure of ships and wine,
You remain mine.
The shrivelled and the fresh stop short,
And the earth stretches forth its head
And pursues us from word to word,
From bird
To bird.

I heard from afar,
And when I tried to approach,
You held up your hand.
I heard from afar
And saw the ancient peoples
There, beyond the woods.

موعد

جَمْعٌ من النساء حول رَجُلٍ محطم .
قلتُ بابتسامة : ندعوه قيس ليلى !
فهَبَطَت الحرارةُ بسرعة .

لم أرَ في حياتي عيوناً كتلك المذَّيلة بالفساتين . وحين تركتُه كان
لا بدَّ لهنَّ أن يلحقن بي .
وانتظرنني هناك امرأةٌ امرأة .
كنتُ في مدينة قرويّة ، غريبة الأطوار، على ضفاف النهر. ودون
أن ابتسم . كان الرجل المحطّم قد اتعبني .
وتمَّ لقائي بهنَّ في البيت القديم فتحوَّلت دعاباتي إلى دم .
وقتلتُهنَّ بالفراغ الكلاسيكي .

أحمد الصافي النجفي

الحرية الخالدة

اقذفوني في الفلا من بعد موتـي
حبذا عيشي وموتي في الفـلاة
لا تزجوني بقـــبر ، انـــني
ابغض السجن و لو بعد ممـاتي

وإذا أصبـــح جسمي مأكلاً
لنسور أو سبـاع ضاريــات
سأرى أجزاء جسمـي سافرتْ
سائحات بيَ في كل الجهـــات

يا لها بعد ممــاتي رحـــلةً
فَذةً متّ عليها في حياتي
كل جُـــزء سائر في عالــم
ناسياً أجـــزاءه المنفصــــلات

74

Rendezvous

A group of women around a shattered man.
I said with a smile: Let's call him Qais, Laila's mad lover.
The temperature sank abruptly.

Never in my life did I see eyes like those with trailing dresses.
The moment I left him they had, of course, to come after me.
And there they waited for me, one after the other.
I was in a rural city, a strange place on the banks of a river.
And even without my smiling, the shattered man had tired me.
It was in the old house that our meeting took place, and my
    jokes turned into blood.
I killed them with classic boredom.

Aḥmad al-Ṣāfī al-Najafī

Immortal Liberty

When I die, cast me forth in the plain:
Sweet unto me there are both life and death.
Confine me not in the tomb:
Hateful unto me is prison, though I be dead.
If my corpse serve as nurture
For eagles and beasts of prey,
Then will I see my dismembered body journey forth
And bear me too in all directions.
O peerless voyage of my dead frame,
In life I was dead to you, unseeing.
Each limb will traverse a separate sphere,
Oblivious of its severed fellows,

وإذا أجـــزاء جسمي اجتمعت

بعد أن طافت جميع الكائنـــات

فسيعطـــي كلُ جـــزء خبراً

ليَ عما قــد رأى من حادثـات

هكذا أفنى وأحيـــا ناقـــلاً

لحياتي من مماتي ، مبهمـات

ان هـــذا لهو الحشـــر الـــذي

وُعد النـــاس بــه بعد الوفاة

بائعة الزهر

جاء ظبي يبيــع زهـــراً جنيّـاً

زاد حسناً بروعـــة التنضيد

قال هلاّ اشتريت منيَ زهـــراً

ضمّ ابهى شقائقٍ ووورود

قلت ابغي شراء اجمـل زهــر

وسأسخو لــه بكـل نقودي

قال لي فاشتر الشقائق تحكـي

أكؤس الخمر أو شفاه الغيد

قلت لا ، قال فاشر ورداً زهيـاً

هو بين الازهار بيتُ القصيد

قلت لا، قال فاشر، ان كنت تشري،

زنبقاً يزدهي ببيض البـــرود

قلت لا ، قال لي اذن فاشر فلاّ

قد حبّوه لون الصبـاح الجديد

قلت لا، قال فاشر النرجس الحاوي

لتبــر في فضــة كالجليـد

قلت لا، قال فاشر آساً ، فلم اقبل ،

فاغضى طرفـاً ومـال بجيد

76

And when again they reunite,
Having travelled throughout creation,
Each will come and relate to me
The happenings it has seen.
Thus will I pass away, yet live again,
Bearing mysteries from the realm of death to life.
This truly is that resurrected life
Promised to man after his decease.

The Flower Seller

A gazelle came selling fresh-plucked flowers,
Their beauty enhanced by artful display.
Her arms full of bright roses and anemones,
She said: "Will you not buy of me a flower?"
I said: "I wish to buy your finest flower,
And will lavish on it all I have."
She said: "Then buy the anemone like unto
A goblet of wine or a maiden's lips."
I said: "No." She said: "Then buy a rose bloom,
Truly the queen among all flowers."
I said: "No." She said: "So buy, if you will, a lily.
Flowering in frigid white."
I said: "No." She said: "Buy then a jasmine,
Gifted with the hue of dawn."
I said: "No." She said: "So buy the narcissus,
That frames specks of gold in icy silver."
I said: "No." She said: "Buy then the myrtle."
I refused, and with narrowed gaze and neck inclined,

قال دعني لم يبقَ عنديَ زهـــر

قلت : باقٍ لديك زهر الحــدود

قال زهر الحدود كم ذا يساوي

لست أدري، فقلت : كلّ وجودي

قال : ما تستفيد من زهر خـــد

نلتَــه في وجــودك المفقــود

قلت : في البيع استفيد هيامــاً

هو عندي يفـــوق كل مفيــد

ان اسمى اللذات ما تنتهي بـــي

لفنــاء ما فوقــه من مزيـــد

لذة السكر تبلــغ الأوج لمــــا

فيه يغدو الرشيدُ غــير رشيد

ان اقصى حدود سـيريَ انــي

انحطى في السير كـل الحدود

نازك الملائكة

« أنـا »

الليل يسأل من أنا

انا سرّه القلق العميق الأسود

انا صمته المتمرّد

قنّعت كنهي بالسكون

ولففت قلبي بالظنون

وبقيت ساهمة هنا

أرنو وتسألني القرون

أنا من أكون ؟

78

She said: "Let me be; I have naught else to offer."
I said: "You have yet the flower of your cheeks."
She said: "For what price would you have it?
I know not." I said: "My whole being."
She said: "What might that flower avail you,
With once your being lost?"
I said: "My gain from the purchase
Is a passion higher than all profit.
Truly the loftiest of pleasures it is
That leads to utter effacement.
The joy of drunkenness is at its peak
When the righteous departs from his path.
The farthest limit of my voyage
I reach after passing beyond all bounds."

Nāzik al-Malā'ikah

Who Am I?

The night asks who am I?
    I am its secret—anxious, black, profound
    I am its rebellious silence
    I have veiled my nature, with silence,
    wrapped my heart in doubt
    and, solemn, remained here
    gazing, while the ages ask me,
                who am I

والريح تسأل من انا
أنا روحها الحيران ان انكرني الزمان
أنا مثلها في لامكان
نبقى نسير ولا انتهاء
نبقى نمرّ ولا بقاء
فإذا بلغنا المنحنى
خلناه خاتمة الشقاء
فإذا فضاء !

والدهر يسأل من أنا
أنا مثله جبارة أطوى عصور
وأعود امنحها النشور
أنا أخلق الماضي البعيد
من فتنة الأمل الرغيد
وأعود أدفعه أنا
لأصوغ لي امسا جديد
غده جليد

والذات تسأل من أنا
أنا مثلها حيرى أحدّق في ظلام
لا شيء يمنحني السلام
أبقى أسائل والجواب
سيظل يحجبه سراب
وأظل أحسبه دنا
فإذا وصلت اليه ذاب
وخبا وغاب

The wind asks who am I?
>I am its confused spirit, whom time has disowned
>I, like it, never resting
>continue to travel without end
>continue to pass without pause
>Should we reach a bend
>we would think it the end of our suffering
>>and then—void

Time asks who am I?
>I, like it, am a giant, embracing centuries
>I return and grant them resurrection
>I create the distant past
>From the charm of pleasant hope
>And I return to bury it
>to fashion for myself a new yesterday
>>whose tomorrow is ice.

The self asks who am I?
>I, like it, am bewildered, gazing into shadows
>Nothing gives me peace
>I continue asking—and the answer
>will remain veiled by a mirage
>I will keep thinking it has come close
>but when I reach it—it has dissolved,
>>died, disappeared.

بدر شاكر السياب

أمام باب الله

منطرحاً أمام بابك الكبيرْ
أصرخ ، في الظلام ، استجيرْ :
يا راعيّ النمال في الرمالْ
وسامعَ الحصاة في قرارة الغدير .
أصيح كالرعود في مغاور الجبال
كآهة الهجير .
أتسمع النداء ؟ يا بوركتَ ، تسمعُ .
وهل تجيب إن سمعتَ ؟
صائدُ الرجال
وساحقُ النساء أنتَ ، يا مفجّعُ
يا مهلكَ العباد بالرجوم والزلازلِ
يا موحشَ المنازل
منطرحاً أمام بابك الكبير
أحسّ بانكسارة الظنون في الضمير .
أثورُ ؟ أغضبُ ؟
وهل يثور في حماكَ مذنبُ

لا أبتغي من الحياة غير ما لديّ :
الهَرْيُ بالغلال يزحم الظلام في مداه ،
وحقلي الحصيد نام في ضحاه
نفضتُ من ترابه يديّ .
ليأت في الغداه
سوايَ زارعون أو سواي حاصدون !
لتنثرِ القبورَ والسنابلَ السنون !
أريدَ أن أعيشَ في سلام :
كشمعة تذوب في الظلام
بدمعة أموت وابتسام .

82

Badr Shākir al-Sayyāb

Before the Gate of God

Cast down before your great gate
I cry out, in the darkness, for asylum
O you who guide the ants in the sand
And hear the pebbles on the streambed
I cry out like thunder in a mountain cave
Like the sigh of the noonday heat
Do you hear my call? O blessed one, you hear
And, hearing do you answer?
                              O hunter of men
Wrecker of women, o torturer
Who efface your servants with cast stones and earthquakes
Who desolate homes
Cast down before your great gate
I feel thought collapse within me
Am I in revolt? In anger?
Does the sinner rebel in your holy shrine?

I desire of life only that which I have:
Darkness crowds the length of the grainfilled barn
While my harvest-field grows in the morning light
I have shaken its dust from my hands
What matter if tomorrow
There come sowers or reapers
Let the years scatter the tombs and ears of corn
I wish to live in peace:
Like a candle melting in the dark
With a tear to die, and a smile

تعبتُ مَن توقّد الهجير
أصارع العبابَ فيه والضمير ،
ومن ليالي مع النخيل ، والسراج ، والظنون
أتابع القوافي
في ظلمة البحار والفيافي

وفي متاهة الشكوك والجنون .
تعبتُ من صراعي الكبير
أشقّ قلبي أطعم الفقير ،
أضيء كوخه بشمعة العيون ،
أكسوه بالبيارق القديمة
تنثّ من رائحة الهزيمة .
تعبتُ من ربيعيَ الأخير
أراه في اللقاح والأقاح والورود ،
أراهُ في كل ربع يعبر الحدود .
تعبتُ من تصنّع الحياة
أعيش بالأمس ، وأدعو أمسيَ الغدا .
كأني ممثل من عالم الردى
تصطاده الأقدار من دجاه
وتوقد الشموع في مسرحه الكبير ،
يضحك للفجر وملء قلبه الهجير .
تعبت كالطفل اذا أتعبه بكاه !

* * *

أودّ لو أنام في حماك
دثاريَ الآثام والخطايا
ومهديَ اختلاجة البغايا
تأنف أن تمسّني يداك .
أود لو أراك .. من يراك ؟
أسعى إلى سدّتك الكبيره
في موكب الخطاة والمعذبين ،
صارخة أصواتُنا الكسيره

84

I am weary of the blazing of noon
Of wrestling with its torrents and my mind
And of my nights with palm tree and lamp and thoughts
Chasing rhymes
In the darkness of sea and desert
In the waste of doubt and lunacy
I am weary of my great struggle
Splitting my heart to feed the poor
Lighting their hovels with my eyes' candle
Clothing them in ancient banners
That exude the smell of defeat
I am weary of my last spring
I see it in the pollen, the marigold, the rose
I see it in every spring, traversing frontiers
I am weary of life's deceit
I live on my yesterday and call it tomorrow
As if I were an actor in the world of doom
Sought out in darkness by the fates
The candles are lit on his great stage
He laughs at the dawn, and his heart is full of the
          noontide blaze
I am weary as a child wearies of weeping

I want to sleep in your holy shrine
Beneath a blanket of sin and error
Cradled in whores' convulsions
So your hands would disdain to touch me
I want to behold you . . . yet who may see you?
I run to your great threshold
In the procession of tormented sinners
Our broken voices crying

خناجراً تمزّق الهواء بالأنين :
« وجوهنا اليباب
كأنها ما يرسم الأطفالُ في التّراب ،
لم تعرف الجمال والوسامة .
تقضّت الطفولة . انطفا سنا الشباب
وذاب كالغمامه ،
ونحن نحمل الوجوه ذاتَها ،
لا تلفت العيون إذ تلوح للعيون
ولا تشفّ عن نفوسنا ، وليس تعكس التفاتَها .
اليك يا مفجّر الجمال ، تائهون
نحن ، نهيم في حدائق الوجوه ، آهْ
من عالم يرى زنابق الماء على المياه
ولا يرى المحار في القرار
واللؤلؤ الفريدَ في المحار ! »

* * *

منطرحاً أصيح ، أنهش الحجار :
« أريد أن أموت يا إلـه ! »

احتراق

وحتى حين أصهرُ جسمَك الحجريّ في ناري
وأنزع من يديكِ الثلج ، تبقى بين عَينينا
صحارى من ثلوج تُنهك الساري ،
كأنك تنظرين إليّ من سُدُمْ وأقمار ،
كأنّا ، منذ كنّا ، في انتظارٍ ما تلاقَيْنا .
ولكنّ انتظار الحبّ لُقيا ... أَين لقيانا ؟
تمزقَ جسمُك العاري ...
تمزقَ ، تحت سَقْف الليل ، نَهْدُك بين أظفاري ...
تمزقِ كل شيء من لَهيبي ، غيرَ أستارِ
تحجبُ فيك ما أهواهْ .

Our throats rending the air in lament:
Our wasted faces
As if scratched by children in the dust
Have known not beauty or charm
Childhood passed, the flash of youth died
And melted like a cloud
And still we wear our same faces
No eye regards them as they pass
They reveal not our souls, reflect not our concern
O exploder of beauty, to you
We wander, straying in the gardens of outward form
Alas
For a world that sees the waterlilies
And sees not the shell on the oceanbed
And the peerless pearl within the shell

Prostrate and biting at the rock I cry
"O god, I wish to die!"

Burning

And even when I smelt your body of stone in my fire
And wrest the ice from your hands, between our eyes
Persist whole wastes of snow that devour the night-traveller
As if you saw me through mist and moonlight
As if we had never met in hope and longing
Hope for love is a meeting . . . where then did we meet?
Your naked body is torn open
Your breasts, beneath the roof of night, are torn by my nails
My ardor has torn apart all but the veils
Which hide within you what I desire

87

كأنّي أشرب الدمَ منك ملْحاً ، ظلّ عطشاناً

مَن استسْقاه . أين هواكِ ؟ أين فؤادكِ العاري ؟

أسدّ عليك بابَ الليل ثم أُعَانقُ البابا

فألْثمُ فيه ظلّي ، ذكرياتي ، بعض أسراري ...

وأبحثُ عنك في ناري

فلا ألقاكِ ، لا ألقى رمادكِ في اللّظى الواري .

سأقذف كلّ نفسي في لظاها ، كلّ ما غابا

وما حضرا .

أريدُكِ فاقتليني كي أُحِسّكِ

واقتلي الحجرا

بفيْض دمٍ ، بنارٍ منك ... واحترقي بلا نارِ !

لاني غريب

لأنّي غريبْ

لأنّ العراق الحبيب

بعيد ، وأنّي هنا في اشتياقْ

إليْه ، إليْها ... أنادي : عراق

فيرجع لي من ندائي نحيب

تفجّر عنه الصدى

أحسّ بأني عبرتُ المدى

إلى عالمٍ من ردى لا يجيب

ندائي ؛

وإمّا هززْتُ الغصونْ

فما يتساقطُ غَيْرُ الردى :

حجارْ

حجارٌ وما من ثمار ،

وحتّى العيون

حجارٌ ، وحتى الهواء الرطيب

88

As if the blood I drink from you were salt
Whole draughts of it still not my thirst
Where is your passion? Where your unbared heart?
I bolt on you the gate of night, then embrace the gate
Conceal within it my shadow, memories and secrets
Then search for you within my fire
And find you not, find not your ashes in the burning flame
I will cast myself into the flame, if it burns or not
Kill me, that I may feel you
                    Kill the stone
With a shedding of blood, with a spark of fire
. . . or burn then without fire

For I Am A Stranger

For I am a stranger
Beloved Iraq
Far distant, and I here in my longing
For it, for her . . . I cry out: Iraq
And from my cry a lament returns
An echo bursts forth
I feel I have crossed the expanse
To a world of decay that responds not
To my cry
If I shake the branches
Only decay will drop from them
Stones
Stones—no fruit
Even the springs
Are stones, even the fresh breeze

حجارٌ يندّيه بعضُ الدم .
حجارٌ ندائي ، وصخرٌ فمي
ورجْلاي ريحٌ تجوب القفار .

قصيدة الى العراق الثائر

عملاءُ « قاسمَ » يُطلقون النارَ ، آه ، على الربيعْ .
سيذوب ما جمعوه من مال حرام كالجليدْ
ليعود ماءً منه تَطْفحُ كلَّ ساقيةٍ ، يُعيد
القَ الحياة إلى الغُصون اليابسات فتستعيد
ما لُصَّ مَنها في الشتاء القاسميّ ... فلا يضيع .
يا للعراقْ !
يا للعراق ! أكاد ألمحُ ، عَبْرَ زاخرة البحارْ ،
في كلِّ مُنْعَطَفَ ، ودربٍ ، أو طريقٍ ، أو زقاق
عَبْرَ الموانىء والدروبْ ،
فيه الوجوه الضاحكات تقولُ : « قد هربَ التّتارْ
واللهُ عاد إلى الجوامع بعد أن طلع النّهار ،
طلع النهار فلا غروب ! »
يا حفصةُ ابتسمي فثغرك زهرة بين السهوب ،
أخذتْ من العملاء ثأرَكَ كفَّ شعبيَ حين ثار
فهوى إلى سَقَرَ عدوّ الشّعْب ، فانطلقتْ قلوب
كانت تخاف فلا تحنّ إلى أخٍ عَبْرَ الحدودْ ،
كانت على مَهَلٍ تذوب ،
كانت إذا مال الغروب
رفعتْ إلى الله الدّعاء : « ألا أغِثْنَا من ثمود ،
من ذلك المجنون يعشق كلّ أحمرَ ، فالدماءْ
تجري وألْسنةُ اللهيب تُمدُّ ، يُعجبه الدمار .
أحرقْه بالنيران تهبط ، كالجحيم ، من السماء ،
واصرعْه صرعاً بالرّصاص ! فإنّه شبحُ الوباء » .

٩٠

Stones moistened with blood
My cry a stone, my mouth a rock
My legs a wind straying in the wastes

An Ode To Revolutionary Iraq

The agents of Qāsim open fire upon the spring,
But all the illicit wealth they have amassed
Will melt like ice, to be again water,
Gushing along streams and brooks,
Bringing back the luster of life to the dry branches,
Restoring, without loss, all stolen from them in Qāsim's winter.
O Iraq!
O Iraq! I can almost glimpse, across the raging seas,
At every turn, in every street and road and alley,
Beyond the ports and highways,
Smiling faces that say: "The Tatars have fled,
God has returned to the mosques with the break of day,
A day on which the sun shall never set!"
O Ḥafṣa! Smile, for your mouth is a flower of the plain,
You are avenged on the traitors at the hands of my people in
        revolt.
The enemy of the people is cast down to the lowest hell,
And freed now are hearts
That feared to long for an exiled brother,
That slowly were dissolving,
And when the day inclined to its end
Raised up a prayer to God:
"Wilt thou not aid us against that Thamud?
That lunatic enamored of every Red?
Blood flows, and the tongues of fire grow long,
Yet death and destruction rejoice him.
Burn him with flames of hellfire falling from the sky!
Cut him down with a bullet, for he is the ghost of death!"

هرع الطبيبُ إليّ – آهِ ، لعلّه عرف الدواء
للداء في جسدي فجاء ؟ –
هرع الطبيبُ إليّ وهو يقول : « ماذا في العراق ؟
الجيّشُ ثارَ ومات « قاسم » .. » – أي بُشْرى بالشّفاء !
ولكدتُ من فرَحي أقوم ، أسيرُ ، أعدو دون داء .
مرحى له .. أي انطلاقْ ! ؟
مرحى لجيْش الأمّة العربية انتزع الوثاق !
يا اخوتي بالله ، بالدم ، بالعروبة ، بالرجاء ،
هُبّوا فقد صُرِعَ الطغاةُ وبدّد اللّيْلَ الضياء !
فلتحرسوها ثورةً عربيّةً صُعِق « الرّفاقْ »
منها وخرّ الظالمون ،
لأنّ « تمّوزَ » استفاقْ
من بعدِ ما سرق العميل سناه ، فانبعثَ العراقْ

مدينة السندباد

جوعان في القبر بلا غذاءْ
عريان في الثلج بلا رداءْ
صرخت في الشتاء :
أقِضَّ يا مطَرْ
مضاجعَ العظام والثّلوج والهباء ،
مضاجعَ الحجرْ ،
وأنبت البذورَ ، ولْتفتّحِ الزّهَر ،
وأحْرِق البيادرَ العقيم بالبروقْ
وفجّرَ العروقْ
وأثْقِل الشّجرْ .
وجئت يا مطر ،
تفجّرت تنشّك السماء والغيوم .
وشُقِّق الصّخَر ،

92

The doctor hurried to my side.
Was it that he had found a cure for the disease in my body?
The doctor hurried to my side and said:
"What is this news from Iraq?
The army has rebelled, Qāsim is dead!"
What joyous, health-restoring tidings!
In my joy, I almost stood up, walked, ran,
As if cured.
Rejoice! What liberation, what release!
Rejoice! The army of the Arab nation has torn off the bonds!
O my brethren in God, in blood, in Arabism, in hope,
Arise, for tyrants are laid low,
And light has dispelled the night.
Guard well the Arab revolution
That crushed the "comrades," cast down the oppressors,
For Tammuz, his splendor once stolen by the traitor,
Has arisen, and Iraq is reborn.

City of Sinbad

1

Hungry in the tomb without food,
Naked in the snow without a cloak,
I cried out in winter:
Bestir, o rain,
The beds of bones and snow and particles of dust,
The beds of stone,
Make the seeds grow, let the flowers open,
And set the sterile threshing floors
On fire with lightning,
Make the roots break through,
And burden down the trees.
And you came, o rain,
The sky and the clouds broke forth to anoint you,
And the rocks were split open,

وفاض ، من هباتك ، الفراتُ واعتكر
وَهبت القبورُ ، هُزَّ موتُها وقام
وصاحت العظام ْ :
تبارَك الإلَه ، واهبُ الدَّمِ المَطَر ْ .
فآه يا مطر !

نودّ لو ننام من جديد ،
نودّ لو نموت من جديد ،
فنومنا براعم انتباه
وموتُنا يُخبّىء الحياة ،
نودّ لو أعادنا الإله
إلى ضمير غيبه الملبّد العميق ،
نود لو سعى بنا الطريق ْ
إلى الوراء ، حيث بدْؤه البعيد .
من أيقظ « العازر » من رقاده الطويل ْ ؟
ليعرف الصباح والأصيل ْ
والصّيف والشتاء ،
لكي يجوع أو يحس جمرة الصَّدى ،
ويحذر الرَّدى ،
ويحسب الدقائق الثّقال والسّراع
ويمدح الرعاع
ويسفك الدّماء !
من الذي أعادنا ، أعاد ما نخاف ؟
مَن الإلـــه في ربوعنا ؟
تَعيش ناره على شموعنا
يعيش حقده على دموعنا .

٢

أهذا أدونيس ، هذا الخواء ؟
وهذا الشحوب ، وهذا الجفاف ؟

94

And, flowing over with your gifts,
The Euphrates muddy turned
The tombs moved, their dead
Were shaken and they arose
And their bones cried out:
Blessed be the god who grants us
Blood in the form of rain
And alas, o rain,
We should like to sleep again,
We should like to die again,
And with our sleep will be buds of awareness,
And our death will conceal life;
We wish the god would take us back
To the heart of his deep, many-layered mystery;
We wish he would lead us backward on the road
To where it has its far beginning.
Who awakened Lazarus from his long sleep?
That he might know the morning and evening,
And summer and winter,
That he might be hungry, or feel
The burning coal of thirst,
And shun death,
And count the heavy, swift minutes
And praise the rabble
And shed blood!
Who revived us?
Did he revive too what we fear?
Who is the god in our dwelling place?
His fire takes life upon our wax candles,
His malice takes life on our tears.

2

Is this Adonis, this emptiness?
And this pallor, this dryness?

أهذا أدونيسُ ؟ أين الضياء ؟
وأين القطاف ؟
مناجلُ لا تحصدُ ،
أزاهر لا تعقدُ ،
مزارعُ سوداء من غير ماء !
أهذا انتظار السّنين الطّويله ؟
أهذا صراخ الرجوله ؟
أهذا أنين النساء ؟
أدونيسُ ! يا لاندحار البطوله .
لقد حطّم الموت فيك الرّجاءْ
وأقبلتَ بالنّظرة الزائفه
وبالقَبْضة الفارغة :
بقبضة تهدِّدُ
ومنجلٍ لا يحصد
سوى العِظام والدّمِ .
اليومُ ؟ والغدُ !
متى سيولدُ ؟
متى سنُولَدُ ؟
٣
ألموتُ في الشوارعِ ،
والعقم في المزارعِ ،
وكل ما نحبّه يموتْ .
الماء قَيَّدوه في البيوتْ
وألهثَ الجداولَ الجفافْ .
هم التَّتَارُ أقبلوا ، ففي المدى رعافْ ،
وشمسُنا دمٌ ، وزادُنا دَمٌ على الصِّحافْ .
محمّدُ اليتيم أحرقوه ، فالمساءْ
يُضيء من حريقه ، وفارت الدّماء
من قَدَميه ، من يديه ، من عيونهِ

Is this Adonis? Where is the glow?
And where is the harvest?
The sickles are not reaping,
The flowers are not blooming,
The black fields have no water!
Is this the expectation of so many years?
Is this the shout of manhood?
Is this the moan of women?
Adonis! Behold the defeat of heroism!
Death indeed has shattered every hope within you,
And you have advanced with a wandering look
and an empty fist:
With a threatening fist
and a sickle that reaps nothing
But bones and blood.
Today? and tomorrow?
When will he be born?
When will we be born?

3

There is death in the streets,
and barrenness in the fields,
and all that we love is dying.
They have bound up the water in the houses
And brooks are panting in the drought.
Behold, the Tatars have advanced,
Their knives are bleeding,
And our sun is blood, our food
is blood upon the platter.
They have burned Muhammad, the orphan,
And the evening glows from his fire,
The blood boiled up in his feet,
In his hands and in his eyes,

وأُحرقَ الالــه في جفونه .
محمَّدُ النبيّ في « حراء » قيدوه
فسمَّر النهار حيث سمَّروه .
غدا سيصلب المسيح في العراق ،
ستأكل الكلاب من دم البُراقْ .

٤

يا ايُها الربيعْ
يا أيها الرَّبيعُ ما الذي دهاكْ ؟
جئتَ بلا مطرْ
جئتَ بلا زهَرْ ،
جئتَ بلا ثَمَرْ ،
وكان منتهاكَ مثل مبتداكْ
يلفه النجيعْ ...
وأقبلَ الصيف علينا أسودَ الغيوم
نهارُه هموم ،
وليله نسهر فيه نحسب النجوم ،
حتى إذا السّنابلُ
نضجن للحَصادْ
وَغنت المناجلُ
وغطّتَ البيادرُ الوهادْ ،
خيّل للجياع أن ربة الزَّهَرْ ،
عشتار ، قد أعادت الأسيرَ للبَشر ،
وكَلَّلَتْ جبينه الغضيرَ بالثمر ،
خيّل للجياع أنَّ كاهلَ المسيح
أزاحَ عن مدفنه الحجَرْ
فسار يبعث الحياة في الضريحِ
ويُبرىء الأبرصَ أو يجدّدُ البصر ؟
من الذي أطلق من عقالها الذئاب !

98

And in his eyelids the god was burned.
They have bound up Muhammad,
The prophet, on Mt. Ḥirā'
And the day was nailed down
Where they nailed him.
Tomorrow, Christ will be crucified
In Iraq, and the dogs will feast
On the blood of Burāq.

4

Oh Spring
Oh Spring, what has afflicted you?
You have come without rain
You have come without flowers,
You have come without fruit,
And your end was like your beginning
Wrapped round in gore; Now Summer
Is upon us with black clouds
Its days full of cares
And its nights
We spend wakefully, counting the stars;
Until that time when the ears of grain
Will be ripe for harvest
And the sickles will sing
And the threshing floors
Will cover up crevices
Then will it seem to the hungry that Ishtar,
The goddess of flowers, has brought back the captive
To mankind, and crowned his lush forehead with fruit?
Then will it seem to the hungry that the shoulder
Of Christ has rolled back the stone from the tomb
Has set out to resurrect life from the grave
And cure the leper or make the blind to see?
Who is this that let loose the wolves from their bonds?

99

من الذي سقى من السَّراب ؟
وَخبَّأ آلوباء في المطَرْ !
ألموتُ في البيوت يولدُ ،
يُولَدُ قابيلُ لكي ينترع الحياه
من رَحم الأرض ومن منابع المياه ،
فيُظلم الغَدُ
وتُجهضُ النساء في المجازر ،
ويرقص اللّهيبُ في البيادر ،
ويهلكُ المسيح قبل العازر ،
دعوه يرقد ،
دعوه فالمسيح ما دعاه !
ما تبتغون ! لحمهُ المقدَّدُ
يباع في مدينة الخُطاه ،
مدينة الحبال والدماء والخمور ،
مدينة الرصاص والصخورْ !
أمس أُزيح من مداها فارسُ النحاس ،
أمس أُزيح فارسُ الحجَرْ ،
فران في سمائها النعاسْ
ورنق الضَّجَرَ ،
وجال في الدّروب فارسٌ من البَشر
يقتِّل النساء
ويصبغُ المهودَ بالدماء
ويلعن القضاءَ والقدَرْ !

٥

كأن بابل القديمةَ المسوَّره
تعودُ من جديد ،
قبابها الطوال من حديد
يدق فيها جَرسٌ كأنَّ مقبره
تئن فيه ، والسَّماء ساحُ مجزره

Who is this that gave us to drink from a mirage,
And concealed the plague in the rain?
Death is being born in houses,
Cain is being born in order to tear out life
From the womb of earth and from the wellsprings of water,
And it will soon be dark.
Women are aborting in slaughterhouses,
And the flame is dancing along the threshing floors,
And Christ will perish before Lazarus.
Let him sleep
Let him, for Christ did not call him!
What do you want? His flesh cut into strips and dried
To be sold in the city of sinners,
The city of rope and blood and wine,
The city of bullets and boulders!
Yesterday they took from its place the copper horseman,
Yesterday they took the stone horseman,
Lethargy reigned in the heavens
And discontent stepped in
And a human horseman pranced through the streets
Slaughtering women
Dyeing the cradles with blood
Cursing divine decree and fate!

5

As if walled, ancient Babylon
had returned once again!
With its high domes of iron
Where a bell is ringing, as if a cemetery
Were moaning in it, and the heavens
The courtyard of a slaughterhouse.

جنانُها المعلّقاتُ زرعُها الرّؤوس ْ
تجزها قواطعُ الفؤوس ْ ،
وتنقر الغربانُ من عيونها ،
وتغرب الشّموس ْ
وراء شعرها الخضيب في غصونها .
أهذه مدينتي ؟ أهذه الطّلول
خُطّ عليها « عاشت الحياه »
من دم قتلاها ، فلا إله ْ
فيها ، ولا ماء ، ولا حقول ؟
أهذه مدينتي ؟ خَناجرُ التتر
تغمد فوق بابها ، وتلهث الفلاه .
حول دروبها ، ولا يزورها القمر ؟
أهذه مدينتي أهذه الحفر
وهذه العظام ؟
يُطلّ من بيوتها الظلام
وتصبغ الدماء بالقتام
اكي تضيعَ ، لا يراها قاطعُ الأثَر ؟
أهذه مدينتي ؟ جريحة القباب
فيها يهوذا أحمر الثياب
يسلط الكلاب
على مهود اخوتي الصغار ... والبيوت ،
تأكل من لحومهم . وفي القرى تموت
عشتار عطشى ، ليس في جبينها زهر ،
وفي يديها سلة ثمارها حجَرْ
ترجم كل زوجةٍ به . وللنّخيل ْ
في شطّها عويل ْ .

Its hanging gardens are sown
With heads cut off by sharp axes,
And the crows peck at their eyes,
While suns set in the west
Behind their hair dyed in branches.
And is this my city? Are these the ruins
On which was inscribed: "Long live life!"
With the blood of its slain?
Is there no god in that place, no water or fields?
Is this my city? Daggers of the Tatars
Sheathed above its gate, and the desert pants
With thirst around its streets, unvisited by the moon?
Is this my city? Are these the pits,
And these the bones?
The shadows look down from their houses
With their blood dyed somber
To be lost and unnoticed
By the pursuer
Is this my city? With injured domes,
in which red-robed Judas
Set the dogs on the cradles
Of my little brothers . . . and the houses,
They eat of their flesh
And in the village Ishtar is dying of thirst,
There are no flowers on her forehead
And in her hands there is a basket, its fruit are stones
Which she casts at every woman. And in the palm trees
On the city's shore there is a wailing.

النهر والموت

بُوَيبْ ...

بُوَيبْ ...

أجراسُ برج ضاع في قَرارةِ البَحَرْ .

الماء في الجِرار ، والغروبُ في الشجَرْ

وتنضحُ الجِرَار أجراساً من المطر

بلورُها يذوبُ في أنين

« بويبُ ... يا بويبْ ! » ،

فَيَدلهمُّ في دمي حنين

إليكَ يا بُوَيبْ ،

يا نهرِيَ الحزينَ كالمطر .

أودُّ لو عدوتُ في الظّلام

أشد قبضتيَّ تحملان شوقَ عام

في كل إصبعٍ ، كَأَني أحملُ النذور

إليكَ ، من قمحٍ ومن زُهور .

أودّ لو أُطلّ من أسرَّةِ التلال

لألمحَ القمَر

يُخوضُ بين ضفّتيكَ ، يزرع الظلال

ويملأُ السِّلال

بالماء والأسماك والزهَرْ .

أود لو أخوضُ فيك ، أتبعُ القمَر

وأسمعُ الحصَى يصلُّ منكَ في القرار

صليلَ آلاف العصافير على الشجَرْ .

أغابةٌ من الدّموع أنتَ أم نهر ؟

والسّمكُ الساهرُ ، هل ينامُ في السّحَر ؟

وهذه النجوم ، هل تظلّ في انتظارْ

تُطعِمُ بالحرير آلافاً من الإبَر ؟

وأنتَ يا بويبْ ...

104

The River and Death

Buwayb . . .
Buwayb . . .
Bells in a tower lost on the seabed,
Water in jars, sunset in trees,
Jars brimming over with bells fashioned of rain,
Their crystal melting in the lament:
"Buwayb . . . o Buwayb!"
And in my blood a somber yearning
For you, o Buwayb,
O river mine, as sad as rain.
I long to run through the darkness
With fists clenched, bearing in each finger
A whole year's hopes, as if bringing you
Pledges of wheat and flowers.
I long to look down from the hills' high throne
To glimpse the moon
Sink between your banks
Planting shadows
And filling its baskets
With water, fish and flowers.
I long to plunge in and pursue the moon,
To hear the pebbles rattle in your depths
Like a thousand sparrows in the boughs.
Are you river, or forest of tears?
Do the wakeful fishes sleep at dawn?
And these stars, do they still wait
To nurture with silk a thousand needles?
You, o Buwayb,

أودُّ لو غرقتُ فيكَ ، القطُ المحار
أشيد منه دارْ
يُضيء فيها خضرة المياه والشّجَر
ما تنضح النّجوم والقَمَر ،
وأغتدي فيكَ مع الجَزرِ إلى البحرْ !
فالموتُ عالمٌ غريبٌ يفتن الصغارْ
وبابهُ الخفيُّ كان فيكَ ، يا بويبْ ...

٢

بويبُ .. يا بويبْ ،
عشرون قد مضين ، كالدّهور كل عام .
واليوم ، حين يُطبق الظّلام
وأستقرُّ في السرير دون أن انام
وأُرهف الضميرَ : دوحةً إلى السّحَر
مُرْهفةَ الغصون والطيور والثمَر —
أحسّ بالدّماء والدّموعِ ، كالمطَر
يَنضَحهنَّ العالَمُ الحزين :
أجراسَ موتى في عروقي تُرعشُ الرّنين ،
فَيَدَكَهم في دمي حنين
إلى رصاصةٍ يشقُّ ثلجُها الزُّؤامْ
أعماقَ صدري ، كالجحيم يُشعِلُ العظام .
أودُّ لو غرقت في دمي إلى القرَار ،
لأحملَ العبء مع البشر
وأبعث الحياة . إنَّ موتي انتصار !

106

I long to drown in you and gather shells
And build of them a house,
And drops of light from the moon and stars
Would suffuse the verdure of water and tree,
And on your ebbtide I would flow down to the sea.
—Death is a strange world that enchants the young
And you held its hidden door, o Buwayb.

Buwayb . . . o Buwayb,
Twenty years are past, each like eternity,
And today as darkness falls,
I come to rest in bed, but not to sleep,
My senses taut like a lofty tree
Stretching its branches, birds and fruit out to dawn.
I feel this world of sorrow
Gushing over with blood and tears, like rain.
Bells tolling from the dead shudder wailing through my veins,
And in my blood a somber yearning
For a bullet whose sudden ice
Will bore the depths of my breast,
Like hellfire set ablaze my bones.
I long to sink to the depths in my blood,
To bear my load with other men,
To resurrect life. Then is my death a victory!

عبد الوهاب البياتي

قصيدتان الى ولدي علي

(١)

قمري الحزين° :

البحر مات وغيّبت أمواجُهُ السوداء قلعَ السندباد°

ولم يعد أبناؤه يتصايحون مع النوارس والصدى المبحوح

والأفق كَفّنَهُ الرماد°

فلِـمن تغـنّي الساحرات° ؟

والبحر مات

والعشب فوق جبينه يطفو وتطفو دنيوات

كانت لنا فيها ، اذا غنّى المغني ، ذكريات

غرقت جزيرتنا وما عاد الغناء

الا بكاء°

والقبّرات°

طارت ، فيا قمري الحزين° :

الكنز في المجرى دفين

في آخر البستان ، تحت شجيرة الليمون ، خبّأهُ هناك السندباد

لكنه خاو ، وها ان الرماد

والثلج والظلمات والأوراق تطمره وتطمر بالضباب الكائنات

أكذا نموت بهذه الأرض الخراب° ؟

ويجفّ قنديل الطفولة في التراب° ؟

أهكذا شمس النهار°

تخبو وليس بموقد الفقراء نار° ؟

(٢)

مدنٌ بلا فجر تنام°

ناديتُ باسمكَ في شوارعها ، فجاوبني الظلام

وسألت عنك الريح وهي تئن في قلب السكون°

108

'Abd al-Wahhāb al-Bayātī

Two Poems to my Son 'Alī

I

O my sad moon:
The sea is dead and its black waves have devoured Sinbad's sail
His sons no more exchange cries with the gulls and the hoarse echo
Rebounds
The horizons are shrouded in ashes
For whom then do the enchantresses sing?
When the sea is dead
And the verdure floats on its brow
Whole worlds floating
Filled with our memories, when the minstrel sang
Now our island is flooded and song has turned to
Weeping
The larks
Have flown, o my sad moon
The treasure in the streambed is buried
At the end of the garden, beneath the little lemon tree
There Sinbad hid it
But it is empty, and ashes
And snow and darkness and leaves entomb it
And the world is entombed in mist
Are we thus to die in this wasteland?
Is the lamp of childhood to smother in the dust?
Is thus the noonday sun to be snuffed out
And the hearth of the poor left mute?

II

Dawnless towns asleep:
In their streets I called your name, and darkness was the answer
I asked the wind after you, as it moaned in the heart of the silence

ورأيت وجهك في المرايا والعيون
وفي زجاج نوافذ الفجر البعيد°
وفي بطاقات البريد .
مدن بلا فجر يغطيها الجليد
هجرت كنائسها عصافيرُ الربيع°
فلمن تغني ؟ والمقاهي أوصدت أبوابها
ولمن تصلي ؟ أيها القلب الصديع
والليل مات°
والمركبات
عادت بلا خيلٍ يغطيها الصقيع°
وسائقوها ميتونْ
أهكذا تمضي السنون ؟
ويمزق القلبَ العذابْ ؟
ونحن من منفى ومن باب لبابْ
نذوي كما تذوي الزنابق في التراب
فقراء ، يا قمري ، نموتْ
وقطارنا أبداً يفوت

سفر الفقر والثورة

(١)

من القاع أناديك
لساني جف واحترقتْ
فراشاتي على فيك
أهذا الثلج من برد لياليك ؟
أهذا الفقر من جود أياديك ؟
على بوّابة الليلِ
يسابق ظلّه ظلي
ويقبع ساغباً عرياناً في الحقل

I saw your face in mirrors and eyes
In the windowpanes of distant dawn
In postcards
Dawnless towns shrouded in ice:
The sparrows of spring have left their churches
To whom should they sing? when the cafes have closed their doors
To whom should they pray? O shattered heart
When the night is dead
And the coaches return frost-coated
No horse between the shafts
Driven by the dead
Do thus the years pass?
And torture rip the heart?
And we, from exile to exile and door to door
Wither like the lily in the dust
Beggars we, o moon, we die
Our train missed for all eternity.

The Book of Poverty and Revolution

1

From the depths I call out to you,
With my tongue dried up, and
My butterflies scorched over your mouth.
Is this snow from the coldness of your nights?
Is this poverty from the generosity of your hands,
With its shadow racing mine at the gate of night,
Crouching hungry and naked in the field,

ويتبعني إلى النهر
أهذا الحجر الصامت من قبري ؟
أهذا الزمن المصلوب في الساحات من عمري ؟
أهذا أنت يا فقري ؛
بلا وجه ، بلا وطنِ
أهذا أنتَّ يا زمني ؟
يخدش وجهك المرآة
ضميرك تحت أحذية البغايا مات
وباعكَ أهلُكَ الفقراء
إلى الموتى من الأحياء
فَمَن سيبيع للموتى ؟
ومن سيبدد الصمتا ؟
ومن منّا ؟
شجاع زمانه ليعيد ما قلنا
ومن سيبوح للريحِ
بما يوحي
بأنا لم نزل أحياء
أهذا القمر الميت انسان ؟
على سارية الفجر ، على حائط بستان
أتسرقني ؟
أتتركني ؟
بلا وطنِ وأكفان
صغاراً آهً قد كنا ، وقد كان ...
لو انّ الفقر انسان
إذن لقتلتُه وشربتُ من دمهِ ،
لو ان الفقر انسان

(٢)

ناديتُ بالبواخر المسافرهْ
بالبجعة المهاجرة
بليلةٍ ، رغم النجوم ، ماطره

Pursuing me to the river?
Is this silent stone from my tomb?
Is this time, crucified in the public square, from my life?
Is this you, o my poverty,
With no face, no homeland?
Is this you, o my time,
Your face scratched in the mirror,
Your conscience dead under the feet of whores?
And your poor people have sold you
To the dead among the living.
Who then shall sell to the dead?
Who shall shatter the silence?
Who among us
Is the hero of our time to repeat what we have said?
And who will whisper to the wind
The hint that we are still alive?
Is this dead moon a man,
On the mast of dawn, on a garden-wall?
Do you rob me?
Do you leave me
Without a homeland and a shroud?
Once, alas, we were small and there was . . .
Would that poverty were a man,
Then I would kill him and drink his blood!

2

Would that poverty were a man!
I called out to the departing ships,
To the migrating swan,
To a night, rainy despite the stars,

بورق الخريف ، بالعيون
بكل ما كان وما يكون
بالنار ، بالغصون
بالشارع المهجور
بقطرات الماء ، بالجسورْ
بالنجمة المحطّمةْ
بالذكريات الهَرِمه
بكل ساعات البيوت المظلمه
بالكلمه
بريشة الفنان
بالظل والألوان
والبحر والربان
أن نحترقْ

لتنطلق
منا شراراتٌ تُضيءُ صرخةَ الثوار
وتوقظ الديك الذي مات على الجدار

سوق القرية

الشمسُ ، والحمرُ الهزيلةُ ، والذبابْ
وحذاءُ جنديّ قديم
يتداولُ الأيديَ ، وفلاحٌ يحدقُ في الفَراغْ :
« في مطلعِ العام الجديدْ
يداي تمتلئان حتماً بالنقودْ
وسأشتري هذا الحذاءْ »
وصياحُ ديكٍ فرّ من قفص ، وقديس صغيرْ :
« ما حكّ جلدَّك مثلُ ظفرِك » و « الطريق إلى الجحيمْ
من جنَّة الفردوس أقربُ » والذبابْ
والحاصدونَ المتعَبونْ :
« زرعوا ، ولم نأكلْ

114

To autumn leaves, to eyes,
To all that was and shall be,
To the fire, to branches,
To the deserted street,
To the drops of rain, to the bridges,
To the shattered star,
To the hoary memories,
To all the hours in darkened houses,
To the word,
To the artist's brush,
To the shade and color,
To the sea and the pilot—
I called out,
"Let us burn,
So that sparks will fly from us,
And illumine the rebels' cry,
And awaken the rooster that is dead on the wall."

The Village Market

The sun, emaciated donkeys, flies,
And a soldier's old boots
Pass from hand to hand,
And a peasant stares into the void:
"At the beginning of next year,
My hands will surely fill with coins,
And I shall buy these boots."
The cry of a cock escaped from its cage,
And a little saint:
"None scratches your skin like your own nail,"
And "the road to Hell is closer than the path of Paradise."
The flies,
And the men tired from harvesting:
"They sowed, and we have not eaten;

ونزرع ، صاغرين َ ، فيأكلون »

والعائدونَ مـنَ المدينة : يا لها وحشاً ضريرْ !

صرعاهُ موتانا ، واجسادُ النساءْ

والحالمونَ الطيبونْ »

وخوارُ أبقار ، وبائعةُ الأساور والعطورْ

كالخنفساء تدِبّ : « قبرتي العزيزة ، يا سدوم !

لن يُصلح َ العطَّارُ ما قد أفسدَ الدهرُ الغَشومْ »

وبنادقُ سودٌ ، ومحراثٌ ، ونارْ

تخبو ، وحدَّادٌ يراودُ جفنَه الدامي النعاسْ :

« أبداً ، على أشكالها تـَقَعُ الطيورْ

والبحرُ لا يقوى على غسلِ الْخَطايا ، والدموعْ »

والشمسُ في كبد السماءْ

وبائعات الكرمِ يَجمعنَ السلالْ :

« عينا حبيبي كوكبانِ

وصدرُهُ وردُ الربيع »

والسوقُ يُقفِرُ ، والحوانيتُ الصغيرةُ ، والذبابْ

يصطاده الأطفالُ ، والأفقُ البعيدْ

وتثاؤُبُ الأكواخِ في غابِ النخيلْ

مسافر بلا حقائب

من لا مكانْ

لا وجه َ ، لا تاريخ َ لي ، من لا مكان

تحت السماء ، وفي عويل الريح أسمعها تناديني : « تعالْ ! »

لا وجه ، لا تاريخ ... أسمعها تناديني : « تعال ! »

عبر التلالْ

مستنقع التاريخ يعبره رجال

عددَ الرمال

We sow, despite ourselves, and they eat;"
And those who return from the city,
O what a blind beast,
Whose victims are our dead,
The bodies of women.
The good-natured dreamers,
And the lowing of cows,
And the woman selling bracelets and perfumes,
Crawling around like a beetle:
"O Sodom, o my dear skylark!
The perfumier cannot repair the damage of oppressive fate."
Blackened rifles, and a plough,
And a flickering fire,
And a blacksmith with a bloodshot eyelid
Lured by sleep:
"Birds of a feather flock together,
And the sea can never wash away sins and tears."
The sun in the liver of the heavens,
And the women selling fruit collect their baskets:
"The eyes of my beloved are stars
And his breast is a bed of spring-roses."
The deserted market, and the small shops,
And the flies,
Hunted by children,
And the distant horizon,
And the yawning of huts in the palm-grove.

Traveller Without Baggage

From nowhere,
With no face, no history, from nowhere,
Beneath the sky, and in the moaning of the wind,
I hear her calling me—"come!"
Across the hills.

The swamp of history crossed by men
As many as the grains of sand.

والأرضُ ما زالت ، وما زال الرجال
يلهو بهم عبث الظلال
مستنقع التاريخ والأرض الحزينة والرجال
عبر التلال

ولعل قد مرّت عليّ ... عليّ آلاف الليال
وأنا ـ سدى ـ في الريح أسمعها تناديني « تعال ! »
عبر التلال

وأنا وآلاف السنينْ
متثائبٌ ، ضَجِرٌ ، حزين
من لا مكان
تحت السماء
في داخلي نفسي تموت ، بلا رجاء
وأنا وآلاف السنين
متثائب ، ضجر ، حزين
سأكون ! لا جدوى ، سأبقى دائماً من لا مكان
لا وجه ، لا تاريخ لي ، من لا مكان
الضوء يصدمني ، وضوضاء المدينة من بعيد
نفس الحياة يعيد رصف طريقها ، سأم جديد
أقوى من الموت العنيد
سأم جديد
... وأسير لا ألوي على شيء ، وآلاف السنين
لا شيء ينتظر المسافرَ غيرُ حاضره الحزين
ـ وحل وطين ـ
وعيون آلاف الجنادب ، والسنين
وتلوح أسوار المدينة ، أي نفعُ أرتجيهْ ؟
من عالم ما زال والأمس الكريه
يحيا ، وليس يقول : « ايهْ »

The earth remains, and men too remain,
The plaything of the shadows.
The swamp of history, the sad land,
And the men,
Across the hills.

There passed over me perhaps thousands of nights,
While in vain I heard her call in the wind—"come!"
Across the hills.

I, and thousands of years,
Yawning, sad, bored,
From nowhere,
Beneath the sky,
Within me my soul dying with no hope,
While I and thousands of years
Are yawning, sad, bored.
I shall be, but in vain!
I shall remain from nowhere,
With no face, no history, from nowhere.
Light and the tumult of the city strike me from afar.
The same life,
A new boredom stronger than stubborn death repaves its road,
A new boredom.

I walk on, caring for nothing.
Thousands of years, and nothing waiting for the traveller
Save his sad present,
Mud and clay,
Thousands of years,
And the eyes of thousands of locusts.
The walls of the city appear, but for what gain shall I hope,
From a world which still lives with a hateful past
Without a sound of protest?

يحيا على جيف معطّرة الجباه
نفسُ الحياة
نفس الحياة يعيد رصف طريقها ، سأمٌ جديدْ
أقوى من الموت العنيد
تحت السماء
بلا رجاء
في داخلي نفسي تموتْ
كالعنكبوت
نفسي تموت
وعلى الجدار
ضوء النهار
يمتص أعوامي ، ويبصقها دماً ، ضوءُ النهارْ
أبداً لأجلي ، لم يكن هذا النهارْ
الباب أغلقَ ! لمْ يكن هذا النهار
أبداً لأجلي لم يكن هذا النهار
سأكون ! لا جدوى ، سأبقى دائماً من لا مكان
لا وجه ، لا تاريخ لي ، من لا مكان

بلند الحيدري

ساعي البريد

ساعي البريدْ
ماذا تريد .. ؟
انا عن الدنيا بمنأى بعيد
اخطأتَ ... لا شك فما من جديد
تحمله الارض لهذا الطريد
ما كان
ما زال على عهده
يحلم

Which lives on carrion with perfumed brows?
The same life,
The same life,
A new boredom stronger than stubborn death repaves its road,
Beneath the sky
With no hope.
Within me my soul dying
Like the spider,
My soul dying.

On the wall
The light of day
Sucks my years, spits them out in blood,
The light of day.
This day was never meant for me.
The door was shut, this day was never meant for me.
I shall be, but in vain!
I shall remain from nowhere,
With no face, no history, from nowhere.

Buland al-Ḥaydarī

Mailman

O mailman,
What is your desire of me?
I am far removed from the world,
Surely you are mistaken,
For the earth holds nothing new
For this outcast.
What was,
Still is, as it was before.
It dreams,

او يدفن
او يستعيد
ولم تزل للناس اعيادهم
ومأتم يربط عيداً بعيد
اعينهم تنبش في ذهنهم
عن عظمة اخرى بجوع جديد
ولم تزل للصين من سورها
اسطورة تمحى ودهر يعيد
ولم يزل للارض سيزيفها
وصخرة تجهل ماذا تريد

*

ساعي البريد
اخطأت .. لا شك فما من جديد
وعد مع الدرب ويا طالما
جاء بك الدرب
وماذا ... تريد
؟

الخطوة الضائعة

كان الشتاء يجز ارصفة المحطة
وتموءُ عاصفة كقطه
وعلى الطريق
يهتز فانوس عتيق
فيهز قريتنا الضنينه
ماذا سافعل في المدينة .. ؟
وسألتني :
ماذا ستفعل في المدينه .. !

It buries,
And tries to regain.
People still have their festivals,
And mourning connects one festival with the next.
Their eyes dig in the graveyard of their minds
Looking for some new glory
To quiet some new hunger.
China still has its wall,
A legend once effaced brought back by time.
The earth still has its Sisyphus,
And a rock that does not know
Its desire.

O mailman,
Surely you are mistaken,
For there is nothing new. . . .
Return along the path whence you came,
The path that so often brings you.
What is your desire of me?

A False Step

Winter's sharp blade cut into the platform,
The storm miaowed like a cat,
Over the rails
Swung an ancient lamp,
And our frugal village
Quivered in its light.
"What will I do in the city?"
She asked me:
"What will you do in the city?

ستضيع خطوتُك الغبية في شوارعها الكبيرة
ولسوف تسحقك
الازقاتُ الضريره
ولسوف ينمو الليل في اعماقك الصماءِ
آمالاً حزينه
ماذا ستفعل في الـ ... وبلا صديق
لا .. ليس في تلك المدينة من صديق
وضحكت مني
وظللتُ انتَظر القطار إلى المدينه
ومضيتِ عني
ومضيتُ عنك
ومن خلال زجاج نافذة القطار
مرت قُرى
تطفو وترسب في الرمال وكنت انتظر النهار
على المدينه

*

ولن اعودُ .. !
لقريتي
او للشتاء يحز ارصفة المحطة
او للضياء يهز قريتنا الضنينه
او للنساء المائتات من الحياء
لا .. لن اعودَ
لن اعود وقريتي امست مدينه
في كل منعطف ضياء
قاس لمصباح جديد
سيصيح بي :
ــ ماذا تريدْ .. ؟
ــ ماذا اريدْ .. !
لا شيء يعرفني واعرفه هنا

Down its long streets
Your ignorant steps will go astray
And its blind alleys
Will swallow you up.
Night will glow in your heart's numbed depths,
And sad longings spring up.
What will you do there, without a friend?
No, there's no friend to be found in a city."
You laughed at me,
And still I waited for the citybound train.
You walked away from me,
And I from you.
Beyond the windows of the train,
Villages passed by,
Rose up and sank back in the sand,
And I waited for morning
In the city.

For whom should I return?
For my village?
For winter's sharp blade that cut into the platform?
The light in which our frugal village quivered?
Or the women dead with modesty and shame?
No, I shall not return.
For whom should I return?
My village is become a city.
At every corner,
A new lamp's harsh light
Will cry out to me:
"What do you wish?"
What do I wish?!
Here, there is nothing I know,
And nothing that knows me;

لا شيء يذكرني واذكره هنا
ساجر خطوتيَ الصغيرةَ
في شوارعها الكبيره
ولسوف تسحقني الازقاتُ الضريره
لا .. لن اعودَ
لمن اعودُ ، فقريتي امست مدينه .

عقم

نفس الطريق°
نفس البيوت ، يشدها جهد عميق
نفس السكوت

كنا نقول :
غداً يموت وتستفيق
من كل دار
اصوات اطفال صغار
يتدحرجون مع النهار على الطريق
وسيسخرون بامسنا
بنسائنا المتأففات

بعيوننا المتجمدات بلا بريق
لن يعرفوا ما الذكريات
لن يفهموا الدرب العتيق
وسيضحكون لانهم لا يسألون
لِمَ يضحكون .. ؟

*

كنا نقول :
غداً سندرك ما نقول

126

Nothing I remember,
Or that remembers me.
I shall drag my short steps
Down the long streets,
And be swallowed up
In the blind alleys.
No, I shall not return.
For whom should I return?
My village is become a city.

Barrenness

The same road,
The same houses,
Held together by profound exertion,
The same silence.
We used to say:
Tomorrow it will die,
And there will awaken
From every house
Young children's voices,
Bursting forth, with the daylight, onto the road
And they will mock our yesterday,
Our grumbling women,
Our dead and lusterless eyes.
They will not know what are memories,
They will not understand the ancient path,
And they will laugh because they do not ask
Why they laugh.

We used to say:
Tomorrow we will understand what we say;

ولسوف تجمعنا الفصول

هنا صديق

وهناك انسان خجول

بالامس كان هوى عميق

ولعلنا ،

لم نعن ما كنا نقول

فاليوم تجمعنا الفصول

ذاك الصديق

بلا صديق

ذاك الهوى

وجه صفيق

وعلى الطريق

نفس الطريق

نفس البيوت ، يشدها جهد عميق

نفس السكوت

وهناك ...

خلف النافذات المغلقات

كانت عيون غائرات

جمدت ،

لتنتظر الصغار

وتخاف ان يمضي النهار

مع الطريق

شيخوخة

شتوية اخرى

وهذا انا

هنا ... بجنب المدفأه

احلم ان تحلم بي امرأه

احلم ان ادفن في صدرها

The seasons will bring us together—
Here a friend,
And there some shy, retiring one.
Yesterday our desires were strong
And maybe we did not mean
What we used to say.
Today the seasons have brought us together—
That friend
Without a friend,
That desire
Impudent and unashamed.
And on the road,
The same road,
The same houses,
Held together by profound exertion.
The same silence.
And there
Behind closed windows
Were the sunken, listless eyes,
Waiting for the children,
And afraid that the daylight
Would pass down the road.

Old Age

Another winter,
And here am I,
By the side of the stove,
Dreaming that a woman might dream of me,
That I might bury in her breast

سراً
فلا تسخر من سرها
احلم ان اطلق من منحنى
عمري سنا
تقول : هذا السنا
ملكي فلا تقربْ له امرأة

*

هنا ... بجنب المدفأة
شتوية اخرى
وهذا انا
انسج احلامي واخشاها
اخاف ان تسخر عيناها
من صلعة
حمقاء في رأسي
من شيبة
بيضاء في نفسي
اخاف ان تركل رجلاها
حبي ..
فامسي انا
هناك ... جنب المدفأة
العوبة تلهو بها امرأة

*

شتوية اخرى وهذا انا
وحدي
لا حب ، لا احلامَ ، لا امرأه
عندي
وفي غد اموت من بردي
هنا ... بجنب المدفأه

A secret she would not mock;
Dreaming that in my fading years
I might spring forth as light,
And she would say:
This light is mine;
Let no woman draw near it.

Here, by the side of the stove,
Another winter,
And here am I,
Spinning my dreams and fearing them,
Afraid her eyes would mock
My bald, idiotic head,
My greying, aged soul,
Afraid her feet would kick
My love,
And here, by the side of the stove,
I would be lightly mocked by woman.

Alone,
Without love, or dreams, or a woman,
And tomorrow I shall die of the cold within,
Here, by the side of the stove.

عبد الرحمن شكري

يا مرحبا

يا مرحبا بالذي يأتي القضاء بـــــــه
حظ المحكم تـــرحيب واعظام

ادر عليّ كــؤوس العيش قاطبة
سعد ونحس واهوان واكــــرام

ان كان عيش فان العيش محتمـــل
او كان موت فما لي عنه احجام

العيش

وما العيش الا ميتـــة بعد ميتـــة
وما الخير واللذات الا عواريا

فيا ليتني كالزهر صيف حياتـــه
فافنى ولم يعنف علي شتائيا

على العيش واللذات مني تحيـــة
والف على موت يريح جنانيا

فمن مبلغ الاموات عني تحيـــة
سلام عليهم بل علي سلاميا

فما اعوزتهم رحمة في قبورهم
كمــا اعوزتني رحمة في حياتيــا

132

ʿAbd al-Raḥmān Shukrī

Welcome

Welcome to the decrees of fate
    for the arbiter merits greetings and respect.
Pass to me all the cups of life:
    joy and misfortune, honor and disgrace.
If I must live . . . life can be endured
If I must die . . . there is no retreat from death.

Life

Life is but a continual dying,
    goodness and pleasures are but borrowed.
Would that I were like the flower whose life is but a summer;
    then I would fade before the afflictions of winter.
To life with its pleasures, from me, one greeting;
    but ah, a thousand to peace-giving death!
Who will convey my greeting unto the dead?
    Peace be upon them . . . nay, upon me:
For in their graves they have no need of mercy
    as I do in my life.

علي محمود طه

أغنية ريفية

وغازلت السّحب ضوءالقمر	اذا داعب الماء ظل الشجر
خوافق بين النّدى والزّهر	وردّدت الطير أنفاسهـــا
تناجي الهديل وتشكو القدر	وناحت مطوّقـة بالهـــوى
يقبّل كل شراع عـــبر	ومرّ على النهر ثغر النسيــم
مفاتن مختلفات الصّــور	وأطلعت الأرض من ليلها
كأنّ الظلام بها ما شعر	هنالك صفصافة في الدّجى
شريد الفؤاد كئيب النّظر	أخذت مكاني في ظلهــا
وأطرق مستغرقاً في الفكر	أمرّ بعيني خــلال السماء
وأسمع صوتك عند النهر	أطالع وجهك تحت النخيل
وتشكو الكآبة مني الضّجر	إلى أن يملّ الدّجى وحشتى
وتشفق مني نجوم السّحر	وتعجب من حيرتي الكائنات
لقاءك في الموعد المنتظر	فأمضي لأرجـــع مستشرقاً

'Ali Maḥmūd Ṭāhā

A Rustic Song

When the water caresses the shade of the tree,
And the clouds court the light of the moon;
And the birds send forth their song
To re-echo between dew and blossom;
And the ringdove laments her passion,
Cooing to her love and bemoaning her fate;
And the lips of the breeze pass over the Nile,
Kissing every passing sail;
And the earth brings forth from its night
Beauties of manifold shape;
And when a willow stands in the darkness,
Hidden as if unknown to night,
There in its shade I take my place,
With heart distraught and saddened gaze.
I let my eyes wander through the skies,
My head downcast and sunk in thought.
Then, I see your face beneath the palm tree,
And by the river I hear your voice,
Until darkness is tired of my loneliness,
And sadness complains of boredom;
Until creation wonders at my bewilderment,
And the morningstar takes pity on me;
And I go on my way, to search again in hope
For our encounter at the longed-for hour.

أبو القاسم الشابي

في ظل وادي الموت

نحنُ نَمشي .. وحولَنا هاتهِ الأكوانُ تَمشي .. لكن لأيّةِ غايه؟
نحنُ نَشدو مع العصافيرِ للشمسِ وهذا الربيعُ ينفخُ نايَـهْ
نحنُ نتارُ روايةَ الكونِ للموتِ ولكن .. ماذا ختامُ الروايَـةْ
هكذا قلتُ للرياحِ فقالتْ : سلْ ضميرَ الوجودِ كيفَ البِدايَـهْ!
وتغَشّى الضبابُ .. نفسي .. فصاحتْ في ملالٍ مرٍّ : إلى أينَ امشي !
قلتُ : سيري مع الحياةِ ، فقالتْ : ما جَنينا تُرى من السيرِ أمسْ ؟
فتهافتْ ــ كالهشيمِ على الأرضِ وناديتُ : أينَ يا قلبُ رَفشي ؟
هاتهِ .. علّني أخطُّ ضريحي في سكونِ الدُجى .. وأدفنُ نفسي
هاتهِ .. فالظلامُ حَولي كثيفٌ وضبابُ الاسى منيـخٌ عليّـا
وكؤوسُ الغرامِ أترعَها الفجرُ ولكنْ تحطّمتْ في يديّـا
والشبابُ الغريرُ ولّى إلى الماضي وخلّى النحيبَ في شفتيّـا
هاتهِ يا فؤادُ ! انّا غريبان نصوغُ الحياةَ فنّـاً شجيّـا
قد رتعنا مع الحيـاةِ طويلاً وشدَونا مع الشبـابِ سنينـا
وعدَونا مع الليالي حفاةً في شعابِ الزمانِ ... حتى دَمينـا
وأكَلنا الترابَ ... حتّى مللْنا وشرِبْنـا الدموعَ .. حتى رَوينـا
ونَثرْنا الاحلامَ والحبَّ والآلامَ والحزنَ . يسرةً ويمينـا
ثُمَّ ماذا .. ؟ هذا أنا .. صرتُ في الدنيا بعيداً عن لهوِها وغناها
في ظلامِ الفناءِ .. أدفنُ أيّـامي ولا استطيعُ حتّى بُكاها
وزهورُ الحيـاةِ تهوي بصمتٍ مُحزِنٍ مُضجِرٍ على قدميّـا
جفّ سحرُ الحياةِ .. يا قلبيَ الباكي فهيّا نُجرّبِ الموتَ ... هيّا ! !

Abū al-Qāsim al-Shābbī

In The Shadow of the Valley of Death

We walk, as all around walks on creation . . . yet, to what goal?
With the birds we sing to the sun, as the spring plays on its flute;
We read out to Death the tale of Life . . . yet, how ends that tale?
Thus I spoke to the winds, and thus they answered: ask of Being
  itself how it began.
Covered over in mist, in bitter weariness cried out my soul:
Whither shall I go?
I said: walk on with Life; it replied: what reaped I as I walked
  before?
Collapsed like parched and withered plant I cried: Where, o
  heart, is my rake?
Bring it, that I may trace my grave in the dark silence, bury myself,
Bring it, for darkness is dense around me, and the mists of sorrow
  are settled on high.
Dawn fills the goblets of passion, yet they shatter in my hands;
Proud youth has fled into the past, and left on my lips a lament.
Come, o heart! We are two strangers who made of life an art of
  sorrow;
We have fed long on life, sung long with youth,
And now with night go barefooted over the rocky paths—and
  bleed.
We are satiated with dust, our thirst quenched with tears,
Left and right we have scattered dreams, love, pain and sorrow,
And then? I, remote from the joy of the world and its song,
In the darkness of death bury the days of my life, cannot even
  mourn their passing,
And the flowers of life, in grievous, troubling silence, fall at my
  feet.
The magic of life is dry: come, o my weeping heart, let us now
  try death. Come!

لويس عوض

كيرياليسون

أبي ، أبي ،
أبي ، أبي ،
أحزان هذا الكوكب
ناء بما قلبي الصبي
الرزء تحت الرُزء في صدري خبي ،
الشوك في جفني ، حراب الهدب
سلت دميعات كذوب السُم من جفني الأبي ،
شبت على قلبي سعيراً مستطير اللهب .
أبي أبي ، أبي أبي ، أبي أبي ، أبي أبي ، أبي أبي
أبكي دموع الناس مختاراً ، ودمع الامس لما ينضب .
لِنْ يا أبي
واستجب
لذي الطوى والسغب
والعاشق المنتحب
واللحم ينعي اللحم تحت الترب ،
والروح يبكي النار تفري عصبي ،
والبشري الغر تحت النير كالثور الغبي .
حولي دماء ورُغاء وهدير غضب
دنياك مأساة أزحتَ الستر عنها منذ بدء الحقب !
طابت لك الرؤيا هنيئاً ! ما أنا الا شقي بأبي .

Lewis ʿAwaḍ

Kiriyalayson

Lord, O Lord
Lord, O Lord
The sorrows of this planet
Weigh down my childlike heart.
Disaster upon disaster, hidden in my breast,
A thorn in my eyelid, with lances for eyelashes,
That draw out of my proud eye meager tears in a poison trickle,
Unleash on my heart a fire of leaping, hovering flame.
Lord, O Lord, Lord, O Lord, Lord, O Lord, Lord, O Lord, Lord,
    O Lord,
I shed the tears of others, for their sake, while those of yesterday
    yet remain.

Relent, O Lord,
Grant the prayer
Of the hungry and the starving,
Of the lover in his lament,
Of flesh mourning the flesh beneath the soil,
Of the soul that weeps tears of fire and rends my nerves,
Of ignorant man, dumb like the ox beneath his yoke.
All around blood, scum and the bellowing of rage.
Your world is a tragedy on which the curtain rose when time
    began.
Enjoy full well the spectacle! Misery is my lot from the Lord.

يا منجبي
يا منجبي ،
قال طال فيك عجبي
لغزك لن يهزأ ني
دنياك قبض الريح ، قالها نبي ،
أخراك آل ذو بريق ذهبي
عبد الرماد وابن دفء البدن المعذب
حنينه للفجر في ليل الشتاء الغيهب
مائدة من نسج وَهْم الطيف آريل البهى المستبى
إنا كأطفال بكوا لما استسر النجم خلف السحب .

الحب في سان لازار

في محطة فكتوريا جلست وبيدي مغزل .
وكان المغزل مغزل أوديسيوس .
عفواً إذا اختلفنا أيها القارىء
فقد رأيتهم ، رأيتهم سكان الأرجو ، وجلهم من النساء ارتدين
البنطلونات ولبسن أحذية من كاوتشوك .
أما نحن ، أنت والفريد بروفروك وأنا
فلنا المغازل نتعلل بها ، وبين الخيط والخيط نرفع أهدابنا إلى الأمواج
في الأفق ، لعل موج الأفق يحمل الأرجو .
وفي الصباح ، عندما يصير موج الأفق موج الشاطىء ، نرى وجه
السعادة .
جلست وبيدي مغزلي في انتظار بنيلوب التي لا أعرفها .
وهل أتت بنيلوب إلى رصيف نمرة ٨ ؟
كلا ، لم تأت بنيلوب إلى رصيف نمرة ٨ .

O my Creator,
O my Creator,
I have for long wondered at you,
Yet your riddle shall not mock me.
Your world is a fistful of wind—as a prophet said,
Your hereafter a mirage with a golden shimmer.
I, a slave of ashes, born of the fever of a body in torment,
Longing for the dawn in the night of gloom,
A spread woven from the fantasies of a ghost, Ariel, luminous
 and alluring
We are like children who weep when the star hides behind the
 cloud.

Love at St. Lazare

At Victoria Station, I sat holding a spindle.
It was the spindle of Odysseus.
(Forgive me, reader, for the change involved).
I saw them, I saw them, the dwellers on the Argosy, mostly
women wearing trousers and rubber shoes.
As for us, that is, you, Alfred Prufrock and myself, we have
spindles with which to while away our time. Between threads,
we raise our eyes to the waves on the horizon, in the hope
that they might be bearing the Argosy,
and in the morning, when the wave on the horizon becomes the
wave on the shore, we might see the face of happiness.
I sat holding my spindle waiting for the unknown Penelope.
Did Penelope come to platform eight?
No, Penelope did not come to platform eight.

هذه الجزيرة العابسة . لقد رأيت الجاريات يدخلن . خلجانها مثقلات .
رأيت الجاريات يحملن الطيوب والخشب والمر .
رأيت الجاريات يحملن العبيد إلى سوق النخاسة في مسقط رأس
ولبر فورس .
رأيت الجاريات يحملن السمك إلى السكا والسكر إلى جزيرة موريس
والقطن والبصل إلى مصر والشاي إلى الصين والافيون إلى الهند
والببغاوات والفيلة وأدوات الزينة إلى القطبين والمترليوزات إلى الصديق
والعدو على السواء .
لكني لم ار الارجو بينها .

صلاح عبد الصبور

أحلام الفارس القديم

نو أننا كنّا كغُصْنَيْ شَجَرَهْ
الشمسُ أرضعتْ عروقنا معا
والفجرُ روّانا ندى معا
ثم اصطبغنا خضرة مزدهره
حين استَطَلْنا فاعتنقنا أذْرُعَا
وفي الربيع نَكْتَسِي ثيابَنا المُلوّنهْ
وفي الخريف ، نَخْلَعُ الثياب ، نَعْرَى بَدَنَا
ونستحمّ في الشتَا ، يُدْفِئُنَا حُنُوّنَا
أو أننا كنا بشطّ البحر موجتينْ
صُفِّيتا من الرمالَ والمَحَارْ
تُوّجتا سبيكةً من النهارِ والزَبَدْ
أسلمتا العنان للتيّارْ
يدفَعُنا من مهدنا للحْدِ نا معا
في مشية راقصة مُدَنْدَنهْ
تشربُنا سحابةٌ رَقِيقهْ

142

This gloomy island. I saw the ships entering its bays, heavy
with freight.
I saw the ships carrying perfume, wood and myrrh.
I saw the ships carrying slaves for the fleshmarket in
Wilberforce's birthplace.
I saw the ships carrying fish for Alaska, sugar for Mauritius,
cotton and onions for Egypt, tea for China, opium for India,
parrots, elephants and cosmetics for the North and South Poles,
and machine-guns for friend and foe alike.
But I didn't see the Argosy among them.

Ṣalāḥ ʿAbd al-Ṣabūr

Dreams of the Ancient Knight

If only we were the two boughs of a tree
The sun would nourish our roots together
And together, dawn would water us with dew
Then we would be tinted with blossoming verdure
When we grew long we would link our arms
In the spring don many-hued garments
In the autumn cast them off, baring our bodies
And bathe in the winter, warmed by our affection

If only we were two waves on the seashore
Pure of sand and shell
Crowned with an ingot of light and foam
Our reins grasped by the current
Driving us on together, from cradle to grave
With dancing, humming gait
A gentle cloud imbibes us

تذوبُ تحت ثغرِ شمسٍ حلوةٍ رفيقه°
ثم نعودُ موجتين توأمين°
أسلمتا العنانَ للتّيارْ
في دورةٍ إلى الأبَدْ°
من البحارِ للسماء°
من السماءِ للبحار°

لو أننا كُنّا بخيمتيْنِ جَارتين°
من شرفةٍ واحدةٍ مَطْلَعُنا
في غيمةٍ واحدةٍ مَضْجَعُنا
نضيءُ للعشّاقَ وحْدَهُم وللمسافرين
نحو ديارِ العشْقِ والمحبّة°
وللحزانى الساهرينَ الحافظينَ مَوْثِقَ الأحبّة°
وحين يأفُلُ الزمانُ يا حبيبي
يُدْرِكُنَا الأفُولْ°
وينطفي غرامُنا الطويلُ بانطفائنا
يبعثُنا الإلهُ في مَساربِ الجنانِ دُرّتَيْن°
بين حصىً كثيرْ°
وقد يرانا مَلَكٌ إذ يَعْبُرُ السبيلْ°
فينحني ، حين نَشُدّ عينهُ إلى صفائنا
يلقطنا ، يمسحنا في ريشه ، يُعجبهُ بَريقُنا
يرشُقُنا في المفرِق الطهورْ°

لو أننا كُنّا جناحَي نَوْرسٍ رقيقْ°
وناعمٍ ، لا يَبْرَحُ المضيقْ°
محلّقٍ على ذُؤاباتِ السُفُنْ°
يبشّرُ الملاحَ بالوصولْ°
ويوقظُ الحَنينَ للأحبابِ والوطَنْ°
منقارُه يقتاتُ بالنَسيمْ°
ويَرتَوي منْ عرقِ الغيُومْ°

And melts in the breath of a sweet and tender sun
Then again we are twin waves
Our reins grasped by the current
In an eternal cycle
From sea to sky
From sky to sea

If only we were two neighboring stars
Rising from the same lofty point
Setting behind the same cloud
Shedding light on solitary lovers and wayfarers
To the lands of love and passion
And on the wakeful sorrowers holding fast to their beloved's pact
When fortune sets, o my love
Decline will overtake us
Our long passion will be extinguished with us
God casting us along the stream-beds of paradise like two pearls
    among pebbles
An angel might see us as he trod his path
And stoop down, his eye caught by our purity
Lift us up and rub us on his cloak, amazed at our luster
And then cast us back into the limpid crossroads

If only we were the wings of a gentle, tender
Seagull, never leaving the strait
Hovering over the ship's wake
Giving the sailor tidings of arrival
Awakening desire for loved ones and for home
His beak nourished by the breeze
Drinking from the perspiration of the clouds

وحينما يُجنّ ليلُ البحر يطوينا معاً ...معا
ثم ينامُ فوق قَلْعِ مركب قديمْ
يؤانسُ البحارةَ الذينَ أرْهقوا بِغُرْبةِ الديارْ
ويؤنِسونَ خوْفهُ وحَيْرَتهْ
بالشدو والأشعارْ
والنفخِ في المِزْمَارْ
لو أننا
لو أننا
لو أننا ، وآه من قسوة « لو »
يا فتني ، إذا افتتحنا بالمُنَى كلامَنا
لكنّنا ...
وآه من قسْوَتها « لكننا »
لأنها تقولُ في حروفها الملفوفة المشتبكهْ
بأننا نُنْكِرُ ما خَلّفَتِ الأيامُ في نفوسنا
نودُ لو نَخْلَعُهُ
نودُ لو نَنْسَاه
نودُ لو نعيدهُ لِرَحِمِ الحياهْ
لكنني يا فتني مجرّبٌ قعيدْ
على رصيفِ عالمٍ يموجُ بالتخليطِ والقِمَامَهْ
كونَ خلاَ من الوَسَامَهْ
أكسبيِّ التعتيمَ والجهامَهْ
حينَ سَقَطْتُ فوقَهُ في مَطْلَعِ الصِبَا

قد كنتُ فيما فاتَ من أيّامْ
يا فتني محارباً صَلْباً ، وفارساً هُمَامْ
من قبلِ أنْ تدوسَ في فؤاديَ الأقدامْ
من قبلِ أن تَجْلدَني الشموسُ والصقيعْ
لكي تذلّ كبريائيَ الرفيعْ
كنتُ أعيشُ في ربيعٍ خالد ، أيّ ربيعْ .

146

Whenever the marine night descends it encloses us together . . .
        together
Then the gull sleeps on the sail of an ancient ship
In company with the sailors stricken by homesickness
They see his fear and confusion
From the singing and the poetry
And the blowing on the horn

If only we
If only
If only we, and o the cruelty of "if only"
O my enchantress if we prefaced our words with wishes
But we
O the cruelty of "but we"
For it proclaims in its intricate twisting letters
That we reject the traces time has left upon our souls
We wish we could remove them
We wish we could forget them
We wish we could return them to the womb of life
But I o my enchantress am a crippled experimenter
On the edge of a world heaving with confusion and decay
A world devoid of beauty
Which granted me darkness and gloom
When dropped onto it at the dawn of childhood

I was once in bygone days
O my enchantress a steadfast warrior, a heroic knight
Before my heart was trodden underfoot
Before sun and frost lashed me
That you might humble my lofty splendor
I used to dwell in unending spring—what a spring

147

وكنتُ إن بكيتُ هزّتني البُكَاء°
وكنتُ عندما أحسّ بالرِثاء°
للبؤساء الضعفاء°
أودّ لوَ أطْعَمتُهُمْ مِنْ قلبيَ الوَجيع°
وكنتُ عندما أرى المحيّرينَ الضائعينْ
التائهينَ في الظلَام°
أود لو يُحْرِقُني ضَيَاعُهُم ، أودّ لو أُضيءْ
وكنتُ ان ضحكتُ صافياً ، كأنني غديرْ
يَفترّ عن ظلِّ النجومِ وجهُهُ الوَضيءْ
ماذا جرى للفارسِ الهُمَامْ° ؟
انخلع القلبُ ، وولّى هارباً بلا زِمَامْ°
وانكسرتْ قَوادمُ الأحْلامْ°
يا مَنْ يدلُّ خُطُوتي على طريقِ الدمعة البريةَ°
يا مَنْ يدلُ خطوتي على طريقِ الضِحكةِ البريةَ°
لك السلام
لك السلام

أعطيكَ ما أعْطَتني الدنيا من التجريبِ والمَهاره°
لقاءَ يوم واحد من البَكَارَه°
لا ، ليسَ غيرَ «أنتَ» من يعيدُني للفارسِ القديمْ
دونَ ثَمَنْ
دون حسابِ الربحِ والخسارَه°

صافيةً أراكِ يا حبيبي كأنما كَبَرْتِ خارجَ الزَمَنْ°
وحينما التقينا يا حبيبي أيقنتُ أننا
مفترقانْ°
وأنني سوفَ أظلّ واقفاً بلا مَكَانْ°
لو لم يُعِدْني حبُّكِ الرقيقُ للطهارَه°
فنعرفَ الحبَ كَغُصْنَيْ شَجَرَه°
كنَجْمَتَيْنِ جارتينْ

When I wept my weeping would convulse me
And I would wish, on hearing the laments
Of the wretched and the weak
That I could nourish them from my grieving heart
I would wish seeing the miserable and perplexed
Wandering in the gloom
That their perdition could set me aflame, that I could shed light
I was carefree when I laughed as if a brook
Whose pure face shows an image of the stars

What befell the heroic knight?
His heart was plucked out and he took to flight dropping the reins
The vanguards of his dreams were shattered
O you who guide my steps on the path of guileless tears
O you who guide my steps on the path of guileless laughter
Peace be upon you
Peace be upon you
I offer you the experience and skill bestowed on me by the world
In return for a single day of innocence
No it is only you who can make me again the ancient knight
Without any payment
Without any reckoning of profit and loss

I see you serene my love as if you had matured apart from time
Whenever we meet my love I know we will part
And I will remain standing in a void
Would that your tender love had not returned me to chastity
Then we would know love like the two branches of a tree
Two neighboring stars

كموجتَين توأمين
مثل جَنَاحَيْ نورسٍ رَقيقْ
عندئذ لا نَفْتَرِقْ
يضمنا معاً طريق
يضمنا معاً طريق ...

أحمد عبد المعطى حجازي

تعليق على منظر طبيعي

شمس تسقط .. في أفق شتويّ
شمس حمراء
والغيم رصاصيّ ،
تنفذ منه حزم الأضواء
وأنا طفل ريفيّ
يدهمني الليل !

* * *
كانت سيّارتنا تلتهم الخيط الأسفلت ،
الصاعد من قريتنا لمدينتنا ،
حين تمنيت ،
لو أنيّ أقذف نفسي ،
فوق العشب المبتلّ !

* * *
شمس تسقط .. في أفق شتويّ
قصر مسحور !
بوّابة نور ،
تفضي لزمان أسطوريّ !
كفّ خضبت بالحناء !
طاووس يصعد في الجوزاء !
بالذيل القزحيّ المنشور

150

Twin waves
The wings of a gentle sea-gull
Then we would not part
A road brings us together again
A road brings us together again

Aḥmad ʿAbd al-Muʿṭī Ḥijāzī

Caption to a Landscape

A sun setting on a wintry horizon,
A red sun,
Leaden clouds,
Pierced by bundles of light,
And me, a peasant child,
Overwhelmed by night.

Our car was devouring the asphalt thread,
Climbing from our village to the city,
And I wished to hurl myself
Onto the moist verdure.

A sun setting on a wintry horizon,
A magic castle,
A gate of light
Opening on a time of legend,
The palm of a hand stained with henna,
A peacock ascending through the heavens,
Its rainbow tail spread out.

في الماضي كان الله ،
يظهر لي حين تغيب الشمس ،
في هيئة بستانيّ
يتجول في الأفق الورديّ
ويرش الماء ،

على الدنيا الخضراء

الصورة مائلة ،
لكنّ الطفل الرسّام
طحنته الأيام !

محمد الفيتوري

الى عينين غريبتين

سيدتي ..
لو لامستْ عينيك هذي الكلمات العاشقات
صدفةً .. لو عبرت خلال الشفتين
فاعتذري عني لعينيك
لأني اتكأت في ظلها ذات مساء
سرقت غفوه ..
داعبت في سكونها النجوم والقمر
نسجت زورقاً خرافياً ، من ورق الزهر
وَسَّدْتُ روحاً متعباً
سقيت شفة لاهثه
أطفأت شوق عين

سيدتي ..
حين التقينا صدفة لقاء الغرباء
كانت كآبتي مثلي ، تمشي في الطريق
عارية بلا قناع
مشقوقة القدم ..
كانت كآبتي أنت

In the past, when the sun was setting,
God would appear to me
As a gardener,
Walking down the pink horizon
And scattering water
Over the verdant world.
The picture is still clear
But the child who drew it
Has been crushed by the passage of days.

Muḥammad al-Faytūrī

To Two Unknown Eyes

Mistress
Should these enamored words chance to meet your eyes
Or pass between your lips
Then forgive me; it was your eyes
In whose shade one evening I leaned resting
And snatched brief slumber
In their repose I caressed the stars and moon
I wove a boat of fancy out of petals
And laid down my tired soul
Gave to drink my thirsty lip
Quenched my eye's desire

Mistress
When we met by chance as strangers meet
My sorrow too was walking on the road
Bare, unveiled
With heavy tread
You were my sorrow

وكان الحزن ، والضياع
كان الصمت ، والندم
يعانقان شاعراً أنهكه الصراع
والشعر يا سيدتي في وطني غريب
يقتله الفراغ ، والعدم
وانتفضتْ روحي ، حين أبصرتك يا سيدتي
شعرت فجأة ، كأن خنجراً يغوص في دمي
يغسل قلبي ، وفمي
يطرحني مخضّب الجبين ، ضارع اليدين
تحت ظلال مقلتيك الحلوتين

سيدتي
لو التقينا فجأه ..
لو أبصرت عيناي تلكم العينين
الأفقين الأخضرين الغارقين في الضباب والمطر
لو جمعتنا صدفة أخرى على الطريق
وكل صدفة قدر
فسوف ألثم الطريق مرتين

ليلة السبت الحزين

الليلة .. الليلة يا حزينة العينين ..
ازدهر الصبّار
فوق قبرنا القديم ، ازدهرت شجيرة الصبار
أضفت على بقايانا ظلالها السوداء
كأنما لم يكفها أنا غدونا غرباء
وأنها تمتصُّ مما نزفت أرواحنا
فنصبت جذوعها من فوقنا صلبان
تكسو بها موتى بلا أكفان
الليلة .. الليلة يا حبيبتي

154

Sadness and loss
Silence and regret
Were embracing a poet consumed by struggle
For poetry, mistress, is a stranger in my land
Killed by emptiness and void
My spirit trembled when I saw you
I felt suddenly as if a dagger delved into my blood
Cleansed my heart, my mouth
Prostrated me with soiled brow and supplicating hands
In the shade of your sweet eyes

Mistress
If suddenly we meet
If my eyes see those your eyes
High-set, green, drowned in mist and rain
If on the road by another chance we meet
And what is chance but fate?
Then would I kiss the road, kiss it twice

Sad Saturday Night

Tonight . . . tonight, o sad-eyed one
The cactus bloomed
Above our ancient tomb, the little cactus
Lavishing its black shade on our remains
As if not satisfied with our estrangement
It imbibes all our souls distill
And stretches above us its hard branches
Covering with them shroudless corpses

Tonight . . . tonight, o beloved

كانت مع السحب عيوني
وانا خلف جداري جثة يسجنها جدار
أكبر مما تبصرين انت يا حزينة العينين
حالك الظلمة .. حالك النهار
يدفنَا .. يحفر قبرنا في كل يوم مرتين
ونحن بعض جثتين
ليس على وجهيهما الا ابتسامةٌ احتقار
وشهقة احتضار
الليلة الدموع .. الليلة الندم
مليون زهرة تسحقها قدم
وجه قتيل يبتسم
شمس تحيض دم
اختلط العذاب بالسأم
القيد في الشفاه ..
والسياط في الجباه
احترقت ستائر الاله
حتى انائي الأزلي .. شاهْ
انائي المقدّس انحطم
يا لفظاعة الألم

عمر أبو ريشة

امرأة وتمثال

حسناء ، هذي دميـــــــةٌ	منحوتـــةٌ من مَرْمــر
طلعتْ عـــلى الدنيـــــــا	طلوع الساخـــر المستهتر
وسَرَت إلى حرم الخلود	على رقاب الاعصــــر !
عريانــة سكر الخيـــال	بعريهــا المتكبـــر
أبـــداً ممتعةٌ بينبـــوع	الصّبــا المتفجـــــر

156

My eyes were with the clouds
And I behind my wall, a corpse imprisoned by a wall
Greater than you perceive, o sad-eyed one
A wall dark by day and night
Buries us, digs our grave twice daily
And we are as two corpses
On their faces but a smile of scorn
And the scream of death

Tonight, tears . . . tonight, regret
A million flowers trampled underfoot
The smile on a murdered face
Blood from a menstruating sun
Torment mixed with disgust
A seal on the lips
A whip on the brow
The veils of God are burnt
Even my eternal cup is defaced
My sacred cup is ruined
O hideousness of pain

'Umar Abū Rīshah

A Woman and a Statue

O beautiful one! Behold this statue carved of marble,
Looking down on the world with cynical disdain
And advancing across the ages to the shrine of immortality.

Naked, intoxicating the imagination with her arrogant nakedness;
Eternally enjoying the gushing spring of youth;

ترنو إليها في وجـــوم | الحالـم المستفسـر
والطرفُ بـــين مُنتَقِل | في سحرهـا ومُسمّر
وشّى بها ، إبداع ناحتها، | الجمـال العبقـري
ومضى ، وبنــت رؤاه | لم تكبر ، ولم تتغيّـــر
حسناء ، ما اقسى فجاآت | الزمــان الأزور
أخشى تمـوت رؤاي إن | تتغيّري ... فتحجّري

طلل

يغيب به المرء عن حسـه | قفي قدمي ! إن هذا المكان
أعاليه تبحث عن أسه | رمال وأنقاض صرح هوت
واسأل يومي عن أمسه | أقلب طرفي بـه ذاهــلا
وتغفو الجفون على أنسه | أكانت تسير عليه الحياة
وتجري المقادير في نحسه | وتشدو البلابل في سعده
وأستنهض الميت من رمسه | أستنطق الصخر عن ناحيته
تكاد تحدث عن بؤسه ! | حوافر خيل الزمان المشتّ
ولا ينعب البوم في رأسـه | فما يرضع الشوك من صدره
تريد التفلّت من حبسـه | وتلك العناكب مذعورة
وباتت تخاف أذى لمسـه | لقد تعبت منه كفّ الدمار
وينتحر الموت في يأسـه | هنا ينفض الوهم أشباحـه

One gazes upon her with the wonder of the questing dreamer,
And the eyes move across her magic, lingering, entranced.
The sculptor's genius made of her an adornment to eternal beauty,
Then passed on, and the daughter of his vision remained, youthful
and unchanging.

O beautiful one! How cruel are the sudden blows of crooked fate!
If you change, I fear that my vision may die . . . so be turned to
stone!

Ruins

Stop! draw near! here indeed is the place where man is driven
from his senses.
Sands, rubble, a castle whose summits have toppled seeking its
foundations.
Dazed, I survey it, inquiring of my today concerning its yesterday:
Did life truly flow over it? did eyelids close over its intimacy?
The nightingales chanted its good fortune—while the fates has-
tened its disaster.
Can I make the stones speak of their sculptors, or raise the dead
from the tomb?
Thorns are not nourished at its breast, nor does the owl croak
over it.
Even the spiders, terrified, seek to escape its prison.
The hand of destruction has tired over it, fearing harm from
its touch.
Here illusion shakes its phantoms, and death kills itself in its
despair.

نزار قباني

البغي

علّقتْ في بابهـا قَنديلَها
نازفَ الشريانِ ، محمرّ الفتيلَهْ

في زقـاق ضوّأتْ أوكارُهُ
كل بيتٍ فيه .. مأساةٌ طويلَهْ

غُرَفٌ .. ضيّقةٌ .. موبـوءةٌ
وعناوينُ (لماري) و (جميلَـهْ)

وبمقهى الحيّ .. حـاك هَـرمٌ
راح يجتـرّ أغانيه الذليلَـهْ

وعجوزٌ خلـف نرجيلتها
عمرُهـا أقدمُ من عمر الرذيلَهْ

إنهـا آمرةُ البيـت هُنـا ..
تشتم الكسلى .. وتسترضي العجولَهْ

وأمام الباب صعلوكٌ هـوىً
تافهُ الهيئةِ .. مسلـوبُ الفضيلَهْ

يعرضُ اللحم على قاضمـه ..
مثلما يعرض سمسارٌ خيولَـهْ

« هذه .. جاءتْ حديثاً سيدي ..
ناهدٌ ما زال في طور الطفولَهْ »

« أو إذا شئتَ .. فرافقْ هذه ..
إنها أشهى من الخمر الأصيلهْ .. »

أيّ رِقٍّ .. مثل أنثى ترتمـي
تحت شاريها بأوراقٍ ضئيلـهْ

160

Nizār Qabbānī

The Whore

She has hung a lamp over her door,
Shedding a light of anemic pink,

In a street full of illuminated hovels,
Where each house is one long tragedy.

Narrow pestilential rooms,
And a name above each door—"Mary" or "Jamīlah."

In the cafe, a decrepit gramophone
Grinds out its wretched songs,

And behind her narghila sits an old woman,
More ancient than vice itself.

She it is who rules the house,
Cursing the lazy, praising the diligent.

Before the door a lusting vagabond,
Banal in aspect, void of virtue.

Flesh is displayed to those who would feed on it,
As the stableman too offers his beasts.

"This one, o master, has come but recently;
Her breasts are full—she is still a mere child.

"Or if you wish, then take that one—
She is sweeter than purest wine."

What slavery like that of the woman cast down—
For mere scraps of paper—underneath her buyer?

قيمة الإنسان مـا أحقرهـا
زعموه غايةً .. وهو وسيلَـه

*

لو ترى الردهةَ فيها اضطجعتْ
كلّ بنتٍ كانفتـاح الزَهَرَه

نهدُهـا منتظـرٌ جزّاره
صابرٌ حتى يلاقي قَـدَرَه

هذه المُذْهبَـةُ السنّ .. هُنا
ترقب البابَ بعـينٍ حـذرَه

حسرتْ عن ركبـةٍ شاحبـة
لونُهـا لونُ الحيَاة المنكَرَه ..

مَنْ سيأتي ؟ من سيأتي معها .. ؟
أي صعلوكٍ حقيرٍ نَكِـرَه ؟

وهنـاك انفردتْ واحـدةٌ
عطرُها أرخصُ من أن أذكرَه

حاجبٌ بولغَ في تخطيطـه
وطلاءٌ كجـدار المقبـرَه ..

وفـمٌ متسـعٌ .. متسـعٌ
كغلاف التينـة المعتصرِه ..

الفُضوليونَ .. من خلف الكُوى
أعينٌ ، جائعةٌ ، مستعـرَه

وشجـارٌ دائـرٌ في منـزل
وسكارى .. ونكـاتٌ قذرَه

مـن رآهـنّ قواريرَ الهـوى
كنعـاجٍ بانتظار المجزرَه

162

How wretched is the worth of man!
They have called it an end; it is but a means.

Were you to see the hall with the women
Prostrate like opened flowers,

Their breasts awaiting the butcher,
Patient, in expectation of fate!

Here, one toothless with age
Watches the door with anxious eye.

She has bared her pallid knee,
Colored with the hue of an evil life.

Who will come? Who will come for her?
What vile and evil beggar?

There sits alone another,
Her perfume the cheapest of the cheap,

Eyebrows extravagantly painted,
Thick powder, like a graveyard wall,

A gaping, wide mouth—wide
As the pressed-out husk of a fig.

The idle stand at the grating—
Their eyes hungry and shameless.

A quarrel inside the house;
Drunkards; filthy jokes.

Who has seen these receptacles for lust
Like sheep waiting for the slaughter?

كم صبايا مثلَ ألوان الضحى
أفسدتهنَّ عجوزٌ خطِرَهْ

*

هذه المجدورةُ الوجـــهِ انزوتْ
كوبـاءٍ .. كبعيـرٍ نتِـنِ
أخرجتْ ساقاً لها معروقةً
مثلَ مَيْتٍ خارجٍ من كَفَنِ
حُفَرٌ في وجهها مُرْعِبةٌ
تركتـها عَجَـلاتُ الزمَـنِ ..
نهدُهـا حبّـةُ تين نشفتْ
رحم اللهُ زمانَ اللـبنِ
فالعصافيرُ التي كانتْ هُنا ..
تتغـذّى بالشـذا والسوسـنِ
كلّهـا طارتْ بعيـداً عندمـا
لم يعُدْ في الأرض غيرُ الدِمَنِ ..
إنها الحمسونَ .. ماذا بعدَها ؟
غيرُ أمطـارِ الشتاء المـحزنِ
إنها الحمسون .. ماذا ظلّ لـي
غيرُ هذا الوحلِ .. هذا العَفَنِ
غيرُ هذي الكأسِ أستهلكُهـا
غيرُ هـذا التبــغِ يستهلكنـي
غيرُ تاريـــخٍ مُدمّـى حيثُمـا
سرتُ .. ألْقى ظلّـهُ يتبعنـي
غيرُ أقدام الخطايا .. رجعتْ
تحرقُ الغرفةَ بي .. تحرقنـي ..

164

How many young girls, each like a hue of dawn,
Has some perilous hag corrupted?

Here stands alone one with pockmarked face,
Like pestilence itself, like a stinking camel,

Her vein-marked leg uncovered
Like that of a corpse from beneath its shroud.

The wheels of time have left
Ruts of terror in her face.

Her breast is withered like a fig,
Its time of milk long since past.

And the sparrows that once were here,
Nurtured on scent and lilies,

All flew far away when only
Ruins were left in the land.

"Now fifty is past; what remains
But the mournful rains of winter?

What remains for me
But this morass, this stench?

This alcohol which I drink down,
This tobacco which eats me away?

A history bloodied wherever I turn,
Casting its shadow behind me?

The footsteps of sin returning,
To burn the room around me, to set me afire?

غيرُ ربّ كنتُ لا أعرفـــهُ
وأراهُ الآنَ لا يعرفـــني ..

*

يا لصوصَ اللحم .. يا تُجّارَهُ
هكذا لحمُ السبايا يؤكلُ

منذ أن كان على الأرضِ الهـــوى
أنتمُ الذئبُ .. ونحن الحَمَــلُ

نحنُ آلاتُ هوًى مُجْهَـــدَةٌ
تفعـــلُ الحبَّ .. ولا تنفعلُ

أنبشـــوا في جثـث فاســـدةٍ
سارقُ الأكفانِ لا يَختجلُ ..

وارقصوا فـــوق نهـــودٍ صُلبتْ
ماتَ فيها النورُ .. ماتَ المخملُ

مَنْ أنا ؟ إحدى خطاياكم أنا
نعجةٌ في دَمكــم تغتســـلُ

أشتهي الأسرةَ والطفلَ وأن
يحتويني مثــلَ غيري .. منزلُ

أرجموني .. سدّدوا أحجاركمْ
كلكمْ يومَ سقوطي .. بَطَــلُ

يا قضاتي .. يا رماتي .. إنكمْ
إنكمْ أجبنُ من أن تعدلـــوا ..

لـــن تخيفــوني ففي شُرْعتكمْ
يُنْصَرَ الباغي .. ويُرمَى الأعزلُ

تُسألُ الأنثى إذا تزني .. وكم
مجرمٍ دامي الزنا .. لا يُسألُ

وسريرٌ واحدٌ .. ضمّهمـــا
تَسقطُ البنتُ .. ويُحمى الرجلُ

166

A Lord Whom I never knew,
And Who—I now see—knows me not?

O thieves of flesh! O dealers in flesh!
It is thus that the hunted beast is eaten.

Since lust has been upon the earth,
You have been as wolves and we, as lambs.

We have been the tortured tools of lust,
Acting out love, impassively.

Exhume our rotting corpses!
Shameless is he who steals a shroud.

Dance over our crucified breasts,
Where all softness and light are dead!

Who am I? I am one of your sins,
A sheep washed in your blood.

Yet I long to be enclosed, like others, by a home,
Enclosed with family and children.

Stone me, aim well your rocks:
You are all heroes on that day when I fall.

You who judge me, you who stone me,
You are too cowardly to be just!

You shall not cause me fear, for your law
Aids the tyrant, stones the weak.

You call the adultress to account,
While how many a bloody adulterer goes free!

But a single bed unites them both:
The woman who perishes and the man thus guarded."

حبـلى

لا تمتقِعْ !
هيَ كلمةٌ عجْلى
إني لأشعرُ أني
حبْلى
وصرختَ كالملسوع بي
« كلاَّ » !
سنمزق الطفلا
وأردتَ تطرُدُني
وأخذتَ تشتمُني
لا شيء يدهشُني
فلقد عرفتُكَ دائماً نذْلا ..

       *

وبعثت بالحدّام يدفعني
في وحشة الدربِ
يا مَنْ
زرعتَ العارَ في صلْبي
وكسرتَ لي قلبي
ليقولَ لي :
« مولايَ ليسَ هُنا .. »
مولاهُ ألفُ هنا
لكنه جبُنَا
لما تأكّد أني حبْلى

       *

ماذا ؟
أتبصُقني ؟
والقيء في حلقي يدمّرني
وأصابع الغثَيان تخنقني
ووريثكَ المشؤوم في بدني

Pregnant

Don't turn pale!
I spoke in haste
But I really think
I'm pregnant
You shouted out as if you had been stung
"No!
We'll tear the child apart"
You wanted to throw me out
Began to curse me
Nothing scares me
For I always knew you were rotten

You sent for the servant to push me out
Into the solitude of the alleyway
You who
Sowed disgrace in my loins
Broke my heart
So that he could tell me
"My master is not at home"
For sure his master is at home
But he became a coward
When he realized I was pregnant

What?
You throw me away?
While I am destroyed by the vomit in my throat
Strangled by the fingers of nausea
And my body holds your cursed heir

والعارُ يسحقني
وحقيقةٌ سوداءُ تملؤوني
هي أني .. حُبْلى
ليراتُكَ الخمسون .. تضحكني ..
لِمَن النقودُ .. لِمنْ
لتجهضَني
لتخيط لي كفَني
هذا إذن ثمني ؟ .
ثمن الوفا يا بؤرة العَفَن
أنا لم أجئْكَ لمالِكَ النتَن
« شكراً » ..
سأسقطُ ذلك الحمْلا ..
أنا لا أريدُ له أباً نذْلا ..

رسالة حب صغيرة

حبيبتي ،
لديَّ شيءٌ كثيرْ ..
أقولُهُ ، لديَّ شيءٌ كثيرْ

من أينَ ؟ يا غاليتي أبتدي
وكلّ ما فيكِ .. أميرٌ .. أميرْ

يا أنت ، يا جاعلةً أحرفي
مما بها ، شرانقاً للحريرْ ..

هذي أغاني ّ .. وهذا أنا
يضُمنا هذا الكتابُ الصغيرْ ..

While I am engulfed by disgrace
Possessed by a somber fact
That I am . . . pregnant
Your fifty liras, they make me laugh
Who's the money for? Who?
It's to get me an abortion
To sew me my shroud
Is then this my price
The price of faithfulness, you heap of filth?
I didn't come for your stinking money
"Thank you"
I'll abort the foetus
I don't want a rotten father for it

A Brief Love Letter

My darling
I have much
To say

Where
O precious one shall I begin?
All that is in you
Is princely

O you
Who makes of my words
Through their meaning
Cocoons of silk

These are my songs
And this is me
This short book
Contains us

غداً ، اذا قلّبت أوراقه
واشتاق مصباحٌ .. وغنّى سريرْ
واخْضَوْضرت من شوقها أحرفٌ
وأوشكت فواصلٌ أن تطير ..

فلا تقولي : يا لهَذا الفتى
أخبرَ عني المنحنى والغديرْ

واللوزَ ، والتوليبَ ، حتى أنا
تسير بي الدنيا إذا ما أسيرْ

وقالَ ما قالَ ، فلا نجمــةٌ
إلا عليها من عبيري عبير

غداً ، يراني الناسُ في شعرِه
فماً نبيذياً .. وشَعْراً قصيرْ

دعي حكايات الناس ، لن تصبحي
كبيرةً .. الا بجي الكبير ..

ماذا تصير الارضُ لو لم تكنْ
لو لم تكن عيناكِ .. ماذا تصير ؟

Tomorrow
When I turn its pages
A lamp will lament
A bed will sing

Its letters from longing
Will turn green
Its commas
Be on the verge of flight

Do not say
Why did this youth
Speak of me to the winding road
And the stream

The almond tree and the tulip
So that the world escorts me
Wherever I go?

Why did he sing these songs?
Now there is no star
That is not
Perfumed with my fragrance

Tomorrow
People will see me in his verse
A mouth the taste of wine
Close-cropped hair

Ignore what people say
You will be great
Only through my great love

What would the world have been
If we had not been
If your eyes had not been
What would the world have been?

خبز وحشيش وقمر ...

عندما يولدُ في الشرق القَمَرْ ..
فالسطوحُ البيضُ تغفو
تحت أكداسِ الزَهَرْ ..
يتركُ الناسُ الحوانيتَ ويمضون زُمَرْ
لملاقاة القَمَرْ ..
يحملونَ الخبز .. والحاكي .. إلى رأسِ الجبالْ
ومعدّاتِ الحدَرْ ..
ويبيعونَ .. ويشرونَ .. خيالْ
وصورْ ..
ويموتون .. إذا عاشَ القمرْ ..
ما الذي يفعلهُ قرصُ ضياءْ ؟
ببلادي ..
ببلادِ الأنبياءْ ..
وبلادِ البسطاءْ ..
ماضغي التبغ وتجار الحدَرْ ..
ما الذي يفعله فينا القمَرْ ؟
فنضيعُ الكبرياءْ ..
ونعيش لنستجدي السماءْ ..
ما الذي عند السماءْ ؟
لكسالى .. ضعفاءْ ..
يستحيلون إلى موتى إذا عاشَ القمرْ ..
ويهزّونَ قبورَ الاولياءْ ..
علّها ترزقُهم رزّاً .. وأطفالاً .. قبورُ الأولياءْ
ويمدّون السجاجيدَ الأنيقاتِ الطُرَرْ ..
يتسلّون بأفيونٍ نسمّيه قدَرْ ..
وقضاءْ ..
في بلادي .. في بلادِ البسطاءْ ..

174

Bread, Hashish and Moonlight

When the moon is born in the east,
And the white rooftops drift asleep
Under the heaped-up light,
People leave their shops and march forth in groups
To meet the moon
Carrying bread, and a radio, to the mountaintops,
And their narcotics.
There, they buy and sell fantasies
And images,
And die—as the moon comes to life.
What does that luminous disc
Do to my land?
The land of the prophets,
The land of the simple,
The chewers of tobacco, the dealers in drugs?
What does the moon do to us,
That we squander our valor
And live only to beg from heaven?
What has heaven
For the lazy and the weak?
When the moon comes to life they are changed to corpses,
And shake the tombs of the saints,
Hoping to be granted some rice, some children. . . .
They spread out their fine and elegant rugs,
And console themselves with an opium we call fate
And destiny.
In my land, the land of the simple.

أيُّ ضعفٍ وانحلالْ ..
يتولانا إذاً الضوء تدفَّقْ
فالسجاجيدُ .. وآلافُ السلالْ ..
وقداحُ الشاي .. والأطفال .. تحتلُ التلالْ ..
في بلادي
حيث يبكي الساذجونْ ..
ويعيشون على الضوء الذي لا يبصرونْ ..
في بلادي
حيث يحيا الناسُ من دون عيونْ ..
حيث يبكي الساذجونْ ..
ويصلّون َ ..
ويزنون َ ..
ويحيون َ اتّكالْ ..
منذ أن كانوا يعيشون اتّكالْ ..
وينادون الهلالْ :
« يا هلالْ ..
ايها النبعُ الذي يُمطر ماسْ ..
وحشيشاً .. ونعاسْ ..
أيها الربُّ الرخاميُّ المعلّقْ
أيها الشيء الذي ليس يُصدّقْ ..
دمتَ للشرق .. لنا
عنقودَ ماسْ ..
للملايين التي قد عُطّلتْ فيها الحواسْ »
                    *
في ليالي الشرق لمّا ..
يبلغُ البدرُ تمامَهْ ..
يتعرى الشرقُ من كلّ كرامَهْ
ونضال ..
فالملايينُ التي تركض من غير نعالِ ..

What weakness and decay
Lay hold of us, when the light streams forth!
Rugs, thousands of baskets,
Glasses of tea and children swarm over the hills.
In my land,
Where the simple weep,
And live in the light they cannot perceive;
In my land,
Where people live without eyes,
Where the simple weep,
And pray,
And fornicate,
And live in resignation,
As they always have,
Calling on the crescent moon:
"O crescent moon!
O spring raining forth diamonds,
Hashish and apathy!
O suspended god of marble!
O unbelievable object!
Always you have been for the east, for us,
A cluster of diamonds,
For the millions whose senses are numbed."

On those eastern nights when
The moon waxes full,
The east divests itself of all honor
And vigor.
The millions who go barefoot,

والتي تؤمن في أربع زوجاتٍ ..
وفي يوم القيامَهْ ...
الملايينُ التي لا تلتقي بالخبزِ ..
إلا في الخَيال ..
والتي تسكن في الليل بيوتاً
من سُعال ..
أبداً .. ما عَرفتْ شكلَ الدواءْ ..
تترَّدى جُثثاً تحت الضياءْ ..
في بلادي ..
حيث يبكي الأغبياءْ ..
ويموتون بكاءْ ..
كلّما طالعهُمْ وجهُ الهلالِ
ويزيدون بكاءْ ..
كلّما حرّكهم عُودٌ ذليلٌ .. و « ليالي »
ذلك الموتُ الذي ندعوهُ في الشرقِ ..
« ليالي » .. وغناءْ
في بلادي ..
في بلاد البسطاءْ ..
حيث نجترّ التواشيحَ الطويلَهْ ..
ذلك السُلُّ الذي يفتك بالشرقِ ..
التواشيحُ الطويلهْ ..
شرقنا المجترّ .. تاريخاً
وأحلاماً كسولَهْ ..
وخرافات خوالي ..
شرقنا ، الباحث عن كلِّ بطولَهْ ..
في أبي زيد الهلالي ..

Who believe in four wives
And the day of judgment;
The millions who encounter bread
Only in their dreams;
Who spend the night in houses
Built of coughs;
Who have never set eyes on medicine;
Fall down like corpses beneath the light.

In my land,
Where the stupid weep
And die weeping
Whenever the crescent moon appears
And their tears increase;
Whenever some wretched lute moves them . . . or the song to
        "night,"
That death we call in the east
Our songs to "night"
In my land,
In the land of the simple,
Where we slowly chew on our unending songs—
A form of consumption destroying the east—
Our east chewing on its history,
Its lethargic dreams,
Its empty legends,
Our east that sees the sum of all heroism
In picaresque Abū Zayd al-Hilālī. . . .

ما قيمة الشعب الذي ليس له لسان ؟

— ١ —

أنعي لكم ، يا أصدقائي اللغة القديمه
والكتب القديمة
أنعي لكم ...
كلامنا المثقوب كالاحذية القديمة
ومفردات الصهر والهجاء والشتيمه
أنعي لكم .. أنعي لكم ..
نهاية الفكر الذي قاد إلى الهزيمه

— ٢ —

مالحة في فمنا القصائد
مالحة ضفائر النساء
والليل .. والاستار .. والمقاعد
مالحة أمامنا الأشياء

— ٣ —

يا وطني الحزين
حولتني بلحظة
من شاعر يكتب شعر الحب والحنين
لشاعر يكتب بالسكين

— ٤ —

لان ما نحسه
أكبر من أوراقنا ..
لا بد أن نخجل من أشعارنا ..

— ٥ —

اذا خسرنا الحرب .. لا غرابه
لاننا ندخلها

What Value Has the People Whose Tongue Is Tied?

1

I bring you news, o my friends,
That the old language is dead,
So too the old books.
Dead
Is our speech full of holes like an old shoe,
Our terms of obscenity, slander and abuse.
I bring you news
That our way of thought
Which led to the defeat
Is dead and at an end.

2

Bitter in the mouth are poems,
Bitter are women's tresses.
The night—curtains—chairs—
Objects stand bitter before us.

3

O my sorrowing fatherland,
In a single moment you changed me
From a poet writing of love and longing
To a poet writing with a knife.

4

What we feel
Is so much greater than these pages.
We cannot but feel shame
At our poems.

5

If we have lost the war, it is not strange,
For we entered it

بكل ما يملكه الشرقي من مواهب الخطابه
بالعنتريات التي ما قتلت ذبابه
لاننا ندخلها
بمنطق الطبلة والربابه

— ٦ —

السر في مأساتنا
صراخنا أضخم من أصواتنا ..
وسيفنا أطول من قاماتنا ..

— ٧ —

خلاصة القضيه
توجز في عباره
لقد لبسنا قشرة الحضاره
والروح جاهليه ..

— ٨ —

بالناي والمزمار ..
لا يحدث انتصار

— ٩ —

كلفنا ارتجالنا
خمسين الف خيمة جديدة

— ١٠ —

لا تلعنوا السماء ..
اذا تخلت عنكم .. لا تلعنوا الظروف
فالله يؤتي النصر من يشاء
وليس حداداً لديكم يصنع السيوف

— ١١ —

يوجعني أن أسمع الانباء في الصباح
يوجعني أن أسمع النباح ..

With all an Oriental's rhetorical gifts,
With empty heroism that would not kill a fly;
For we entered it
With the logic of the drum and the rebab.

6

The secret of our tragedy
Is that our cries are stronger than our voices
And our swords taller than our stature.

7

The essence of the matter,
Summed up in a phrase:
We have donned the husk of civilization,
Yet our soul remains primitive.

8

With pipe and flute,
No victory is won.

9

We have paid for our love of improvision
With fifty thousand new tents.

10

Do not curse the heavens
If they have abandoned you, do not curse circumstance,
For God grants victory to whom He wills,
Not to your blacksmith fashioning swords.

11

It pains me to hear the morning news,
It pains me to hear the dogs barking.

— ١٢ —

ما دخل اليهود من حدودنا ..
وانما تربوا
كالنمل .. من عيوبنا ..

— ١٣ —

خمسة آلاف سنة ..
ونحن في السرداب
ذقوننا طويلة .. نقودنا مجهولة
عيوننا موانىء الذباب ..
يا أصدقائي ..
جربوا ان تكسروا الابواب
ان تغسلوا افكاركم وتغسلوا الاثواب ..
يا أصدقائي ..
جربوا ان تقرأوا كتاب
ان تكتبوا كتاب ..
ان تزرعوا الحروف والرمان والاعناب
ان تبحروا إلى بلاد الثلج والضباب ..
فالناس يجهلونكم
في خارج السرداب
الناس يحسبونكم
نوعاً من الذئاب

— ١٤ —

جلودنا ميتة ا لاحساس
أرواحنا تشكو من الافلاس
أيامنا تدور بين الزار .. والشطرنج والنعاس
هل نحن (خير امة قد اخرجت للناس) ؟

— ١٥ —

كان بوسع نفطنا الدافق في الصحاري ..
ان يستحيل خنجراً من لهب ونار

184

12

The Jews did not cross our borders;
Rather they crept in,
Like ants,
Through the aperture of our faults.

13

For five thousand years
We have been underground.
Our beards are long, our names unknown,
Our eyes harbors for the flies.
O my friends,
Try to break down the doors,
To cleanse your thoughts, your clothes.
O my friends,
Try to read a book,
To write a book,
To sow letters, like grapes and pomegranates,
To voyage to the land of snow and mist.
For you are unknown
To those above ground.
You are thought to be
Some kind of wolf.

14

Our skins are numbed, unfeeling,
Our souls lament their bankruptcy,
Our days pass in witchcraft, chess and slumber.
Are we that "best of all communities raised up for mankind"?

15

Our oil gushing forth in the desert
Might have been a dagger of flame and fire.

لكنه ، واخجلة الاشراف من قريش
وخجلة الاحرار من اوس ومن نزار
يراق تحت ارجل الجواري .

— ١٦ —

نركض في الشوارع
نحمل تحت ابطنا الحبالا
نمارس السحل .. بلا تبصر
نحطم الزجاج والاقفالا ..
نشتم كالضفادع .. نمدح كالضفادع
نجعل من اقزامنا ابطالا ..
نجعل من اشرافنا انذالا
نرتجل البطولة ارتجالا ..
نقعد في الجوامع تنابلا .. كسالى
نشطر الابيات .. او نؤلف الامثال ..
ونشحذ النصر على عدونا
من عنده تعالى ..

— ١٧ —

لو أحد يمنحني الامان ..
لو كنت استطيع ان اقابل السلطان
قلت له : يا سيدي السلطان
كلابك المفترسات مزقت ردائي ..
ومخبروك دائماً ورائي ..
عيونهم ورائي ..
انوفهم ورائي .. اقدامهم ورائي
كالقدر المحتوم كالقضاء ..
يستجوبون زوجي
ويكتبون عندهم اسماء اصدقائي
يا حضرة السلطان
لانني اقتربت من أسوارك الصماء

186

But—o shame of the nobles of Quraysh!
O shame of the valiant men of Aws and of Nizār!—
It flowed away under your concubines' legs.

16

We run through the streets,
Carrying ropes under our arms,
Screaming, without understanding.
We break windows and locks,
Curse like frogs, praise like frogs,
Make heroes out of dwarves,
Make the noble among us, vile,
Improvise heroism,
Sit lazy and listless in the mosques,
Composing verses and compiling proverbs,
And begging for victory over the foe
From His Almighty presence.

17

If my safety were promised me
And I could meet the Sultan,
I would say to him: o Sultan, o my lord!
Your hunting dogs have torn my cloak,
Your spies pursue me without cease,
Their eyes pursue me,
Their noses, their feet,
Like destiny, like fate ineluctable.
They interrogate my wife,
Write down the names of my friends.
O Sultan, o your majesty,
Because I approached your deaf walls,

لاني حاولت ان اكشف عن حزني وعن بلائي
ضربت بالحذاء ..
ارغمني جندك ان آكل من حذائي ..
يا سيدي . يا سيدي السلطان
لقد خسرت الحرب مرتين
لان نصف شعبنا ليس له لسان
ما قيمة الشعب الذي ليس له لسان ؟
لان نصف شعبنا محاصر كالنمل والجرذان
في داخل الجدران ..
لو احد يمنحني الامان من عسكر السلطان
قلت له : لقد خسرت الحرب مرتين
لانك انفصلت عن قضية الانسان .

— ١٨ —

لو اننا لم ندفن الوحدة في التراب
لو لم نمزق جسمها الطري بالحراب
لو بقيت في داخل العيون والاهداب
لما استباحت لحمنا الكلاب .

— ١٩ —

نريد جيلا غاضبا
نريد جيلا يفلح الافاق
وينكش التاريخ من جذوره
وينكش الفكر من الاعماق
نريد جيلا قادما مختلف الملامح
لا يغفر الاخطاء . لا يسامح
لا ينحني . لا يعرف النفاق
نريد جيلا ، رائداً ، عملاق .

— ٢٠ —

يا ايها الاطفال ..
من المحيط للخليج ، انتم سنابل الآمال

Hoping to reveal my sadness and my plight,
I was beaten with my shoes.
Your soldiers forced this shame upon me.
O Sultan, o my lord,
You have lost the war twice
Because half our people has no tongue—
And what value has the people whose tongue is tied?
Because half our people are imprisoned like ants and rats,
Enclosed in walls.
If I were promised safety
From the soldiers of the Sultan,
I would say to him: you have lost the war twice
Because you have abandoned the cause of man.

18

If we had not buried our unity in the dust,
And not torn its fragile body with our spears,
If it had stayed well-guarded in our eyes—
The dogs would not now be feasting on our flesh.

19

We need an angry generation,
A generation to plough the horizons,
To pluck up history from its roots,
To wrench up our thought from its foundations.
We need a generation of different mien
That forgives no error, is not forbearing,
That falters not, knows no hypocrisy.
We need a whole generation of leaders and of giants.

20

O children
From Atlantic Ocean to Arabian Gulf,
You are our hope like ears of corn,

وانتم الجيل الذي سيكسر الاغلال
ويقتل الافيون في رؤوسنا ..
ويقتل الخيال
يا ايها الاطفال انتم بعد طيبون
وطاهرون ، كالندى والثلج ، طاهرون
لا تقرأوا عن جيلنا المهزوم يا أطفال
فنحن خائبون
ونحن ، مثل قشرة البطيخ ، تافهون
ونحن منخورون .. منخورون .. كالنعال
لا تقرأوا اخبارنا .. لا تقتنوا آثارنا
لا تقبلوا افكارنا
فنحن جيل القيء ، والزهري ، والسعال
ونحن جيل الدجل ، والرقص على الحبال
يا ايها الاطفال ...
يا مطر الربيع
يا سنابل الآمال ...
انتم بذور الخصب في حياتنا العقيمة
وانتم الجيل الذي سيهزم
الهزيمة ...

الى قديسة ..

ماذا إذن تتوقعين ؟
يا بضعة امرأة .. أجيبي
ما الذي تتوقعين ؟
أظلّ أصطاد الذباب هنا ؟
وأنت تدخّنين ..
أجترّ كالحشّاش أحلامي
وأنت تدخّنين ..

You are the generation that will break the fetters
And will kill the opium in our heads,
Will kill our illusions.
O children, you are still sound
And pure, like dew or snow.
Do not follow our defeated generation,
For we have failed,
Are worthless and banal as a melon-rind,
Are rotten as a worn-out sandal.
Do not read our history, do not trace our deeds,
Do not embrace our thoughts,
For we are the generation of nausea, of syphilis and consumption,
We are the generation of deception and tightrope-walking.
O children,
O rain of spring,
O saplings of hope,
You are the fertile seeds in our barren life,
You are the generation that will vanquish
The defeat.

To A Saint

What then do you expect?
Tell me, o hunk of woman
What do you expect?
Shall I keep on chasing flies
While you smoke?
Chew on my dreams like a hashish addict
While you smoke?

وأنا

أمام سريرك الزاهي كقط مسكين

ماتت مخالبه وعزّته .. وهدّته السنين

أنا لن أكون ـ تأكّدي ـ

القطّ الذي تتصوّرين ..

قطّا من الخشب المجوّف لا يحركه الحنين

يغفو على الكرسيّ إذ تتجرّدين ..

ويردّ عينيه ..

اذا انحسرت قباب الياسمين

* * *

تلك النهاية .. ليس تدهشني

فمالك تدهشين

هذا انا ..

هذا الذي عندي ..

فماذا تأمرين ؟

أعصابي احترقت ..

وأنت على سريرك تقرأين

أأصوم عن شفتيك ؟

فوق رجولتي ما تطلبين ..

ما حكمتي ؟

ما طيبتي ؟

هذا طعام الميتين ..

* * *

متصوّف !

من قال ؟ إني آخر المتصوفين ..

أنا لست يا قديستي الرب الذي تتخيلين ..

رجل أنا كالآخرين ..

بطهارتي ..

بنذالتي

192

And I
In front of your resplendent bed
Am like a wretched cat
His claws and his honor dead
Destroyed by the years
Be sure I shan't be
The cat you imagine
A hollow wooden cat unmoved by feeling
Dozing on the chair while you undress
Turning away his eyes
When the jasmine domes are revealed

That ending doesn't scare me
Why then are you scared?
This is me
This is what I have
What then are your orders?
My nerves are burnt up
And you lie reading on your bed
Must I vow a fast on your lips?
What you ask is too much for my virility.
My wisdom?
My goodness?
Food for the dead!

A Sufi!
Who said it? Me, the last of the Sufis!
I am not, o "saint," the god whom you imagine
But a man like others
In purity
And in vice

رجل أنا كالآخرين ..
فيه مزايا الأنبياء ..
وفيه كفر الكافرين ..
ووداعة الأطفال فيه .. وقسوة المتوحشين

* * *

رجل أنا كالآخرين ....
رجل يحبّ ‐ إذا أحبّ ‐
بكل عنف الأربعين
لو كنت يوماً تفهمين ..
ما الأربعون ؟
وما الذي يعنيه حبّ الأربعين ..
يا بضعة امرأة
لو أنك تفهمين ..

أدونيس (علي أحمد سعيد)

العصفور

أصغيتُ :
عصفورٌ على صنّين
يَضجُّ كي تسيطرَ السّكينه
كي يُصبح الغناءُ
كشفرة السّكّين
يجرحُ بالبحّة والبُكاء
برودةَ المدينه .

الدم النافر

أحلمُ :
لن يكون هذا الصّوتْ

With the virtues of the prophets
And the heresy of the infidels
The gentleness of a child
And the cruelty of a savage

I am a man like others
A man who loves—when he does—
With all the violence of forty years
If only you understood
What that means, forty years
And what too the love of forty years
O hunk of woman
If only you understood.

ʿAlī Aḥmad Saʿīd (Adonis)

The Bird
A Dream

I listened:
A bird on Mount Ṣinnīn
Singing on and on
Until silence prevails,
Until its song becomes like
The blade of a knife,
Wounding, with hoarseness and weeping,
The city's chill.

The Gushing Blood
A Dream

I dream:
This voice will never be

صوتيَ ،
أنتَ الجثّةُ الطّريحه'
أنا الدَّم النّافرُ من حضارةٍ ذبيحَه'
يُشعِلُ نارَ الموتْ
يُطفىء نارَ الموتْ .

الشهيد

حين رأيتُ اللّيلَ في جفونِه الملتهبة
ولم أجد في وجهه نخيلاً
ولم أجدْ نجوماً ،
عَصفتُ حولَ رأسه
كالرّيحِ — وانكسرتُ مثلَ قَصَبَه' .

حوار

— « لا تَقُلْ كانْ حيّ
خاتماً أو سِوارْ
إنّ حيي حصارْ
إنّه الجامحون'
يُبحرون إلى موتِهم ، يَبحثون' ...
لا تقلْ كان حي
قمراً ،
إنّه شَرارْ . »

المئذنة

بكت المئذنــه'
حينَ جاء الْغريبُ — اشتَراها
وبنى فوقها مدخنه .

196

My voice.
You are the corpse outstretched—
I am the blood gushing from a slaughtered civilization,
Kindling the fire of death,
Quenching the fire of death.

The Martyr

When I saw the night in his blazing eyelids
And found no palm trees in his face
And no stars,
Like the wind, I whirled
Around his head—
Like a reed, I broke.

Dialogue

Do not say my love was
A ring or a bracelet.
My love is a siege,
Is the daring and headstrong
Who, searching, sail out to their death.

Do not say my love was
A moon.
My love is a burst of sparks.

The Minaret
A Dream

The minaret wept
When the stranger came, bought it,
And over it built a chimney.

الغرب والشرق

كان شيءٌ يمتدُّ في نفَق التَّاريخ
شيء مزيَّنٌ ملغومُ
حاملاً طفلَه من النَّفْطِ مسموماً
يغنّيه تاجرٌ مسْمومْ
كان َشرْقٌ كالطّفل يسأل ،
يستصرخُ
والْغربُ شيخُه المعصومُ —
بُدِّلت هذه الخريطةُ
فالكونُ حريقٌ
والشّرقُ والْغربُ قبرٌ
واحدٌ
من رمادِه ملمومُ ...؛

محمد الماغوط

من العتبة الى السماء

الآن
والمطر الحزين
يغمر وجهي الحزين
أحلم بسلَّم من الغبار
من الظهور المحدودبة
والراحات المضغوطة على الركب
لأصعد إلى أعالي السماء
وأعرف
أين تذهب آهاتنا وصلواتنا ؟
آه يا حبيبي
لا بد أن تكون
كلّ الآهات والصلوات

West and East
A Dream

There was something stretched along history's buried path,
Something adorned but charged,
Bearing its poisoned infant of oil,
With a poisonous merchant singing his luring song.

There was an East that like a child
Begged and cried for help,
With the West as its unerring master.
The map has been changed;
The whole world is aflame,
And in its ashes
East and West are gathered
In a single tomb.

Muḥammad al-Māghūṭ

From the Doorstep to Heaven

Now,
With the sad rain
Drenching my sad face,
I dream of a ladder of dust,
Collected from hunched backs
And hands clinging onto knees,
To mount to highest heaven
And discover
What becomes of our prayers and sighs.

O my beloved,
All the prayers and sighs,
All the laments and cries for help,

كلّ التنهدات والاستغاثات المنطلقة
من ملايين الافواه والصدور
وعبر آلاف السنين والقرون
متجمعة في مكان ما من السماء ... كالغيوم
ولربما
كانت كلماتي الآن
قرب كلمات المسيح
فلننتظر بكاء السماء
يا حبيبي

حلم

منذ أن خلق البرد والابواب المغلقة
وأنا أمدّ يدي كالأعمى
بحثا عن جدار
أو امرأة تؤويني
ولكن ماذا تفعل الغزالة العمياء
بالنبع الجاري؟
والبلبل الاسير
بالأفق الذي يلامس قضبانه؟
في عصر الذرة والعقول الالكترونية
في زمن العطر والغناء والأضواء الخافتة
كنت أحدثها عن حداء البدو
والسفر إلى الصحراء
على ظهور الجمال
ونهداها يصغيان إلي
كما يصغي الاطفال الصغار
لحديث ممتع حول الموقد
كنا نحلم بالصحراء

Springing from
Millions of lips and hearts,
Through thousands of years and centuries,
Must be gathered somewhere in heaven,
Like clouds.
And maybe
These words of mine
Are now close to those of Jesus.
So let us await the tears of heaven,
O beloved.

Dream

Since cold and closed doors were created,
I, like the blind, have stretched out my hands,
Searching for a wall
Or a woman to shelter me.
But what can the blind gazelle do with a flowering spring?
The captive nightingale with the horizon which brushes the bars
        of his cage?

In the age of the atom and the electronic brain,
In the time of perfume, soft light and song,
I told her of Bedouin chanting,
Of journeying to the desert
On camelback,
And her young breasts listened to me,
As little children sitting around a fire
Listen to a charming tale.
We were dreaming of the desert

كما يحلم الراهب بالمضاجعة
واليتيم بالمزمار
وكنت أقول لها وأنا أرسل
نظراتي إلى الافق البعيد :
هناك نتكىء على الرمال الزرقاء
وننام صامتين حتى الصباح
لا لأن الكلمات قليلة
ولكن لأن الفراشات المتعبة
تنام على شفاهنا .
غداً يا حبيبتي غدا
نستيقظ مبكرين
مع الملاحين وأشرعة البحر
ونرتفع مع الريح كالطيور
كالدماء عند الغضب
ونهوي على الصحراء
كما يهوي الفم على الفم
وننما متعانقين طوال الليل
وأيدينا على حقائبنا
وفي الصباح أقلعنا عن السفر
لأن الصحراء كانت في قلبينا .

فدوى طوقان

لن أبيع حبه

أيّ صدفه
صدفة كالحلم حلوه
جمعتنا ههنا في هذه الارض القصيّة
نحن روحان غريبان هنا
ألّفت ما بيننا

As the monk dreams of a woman's arms,
And the orphan, of a flute.

I said to her, as I cast my gaze
On the distant horizon:
There on the blue sands we will lie
And sleep silently till daybreak,
Not for want of words,
But because the weary butterflies
Will be sleeping on our lips.
Tomorrow, o beloved, tomorrow
We will awaken early with the sailors and their sails,
And we will rise on the wind
Like birds,
Like raging blood,
And roam over the desert
As lips roam over lips.
Locked in embrace, we slept throughout the night,
Our hands upon our baggage.
And in the morning
We renounced our journey
For the desert was in our hearts.

Fadwā Ṭūqān

I Won't Sell His Love

What chance
Sweet dreamlike chance
Joined us here in this distant land
Here two strange souls we
Were united by the Muse

ربّة الفن ، وقد طافت بنا
فاذا الروحان غنوه
سبحت في لحن (موزارت) ودنياه الغنيه

قلتَ : في عينيكِ عمق،
انت حلوه
قلتهاً في رغبة مهموسة الجرس —
انه ابن بلادي لن ابيع
حبـــه
بكنوز الارضِ
بالانجم زهراً
بالقمر
غير أنيّ تعتري قلبي نشوه
فما كنّا بخلوه
وبعينيكَ نداء
وبأعماقيَ نشوه
ايّ نشوه
انا انثى فاغتفر للقلب زهوه
كلما دغدغه همسك : في عينيك عمق
انت حلوه

انا يا شاعر لي في وطني
وطني الغالي حبيبٌ ينتظر
انه ابن بلادي لن اضيع
قلبـــه
حينما تطفو ظلال الحب في عينيك
او تومض دعوه
انا انثى ، فاغتفر للقلب زهوه
كلما دغدغه همسك : في عينيك عمق
انت حلوه

Who carried us away
Our souls becoming a song
Floating on a Mozart air
In its precious world

You said: How deep your eyes
How sweet you are
You said it with hushed, echoing desire
For we were not alone
And in your eyes an invitation
And in my depths intoxication
What intoxication
I am a woman so forgive my heart its vanity
When your murmur caresses it: How deep your eyes
How sweet you are

O Poet, in my country
My beloved country
I have a sweetheart waiting
He is my countryman I won't squander
His heart
He is my countryman I won't sell
His love
For the world's treasures
For the shining stars
For the Moon
Yet intoxication grips my heart
As in your eyes drift love's shadows
Or invitation glimmers
I am a woman so forgive my heart its vanity
When your murmur caresses it: How deep your eyes
How sweet you are

سلمى الخضراء الجيوسي

مرثية الشهداء

أنا أدري أنهم ماتوا « ليحيا الوطن »
وطن القتلى وحقل الدم هذا الوطن
أنا أدري أنها « الحرية الحمراء » هذا الثمن
الرائع ، المغموس بالآهات ، هذا الثمن ..
أنا أدري .. إنما الحزن بأعماق فؤادي ليس يدري ،
أنا أبكي كلّ عين فقدت ضوء الحياه
كل روح سال من بين الشفاه

* * *

فاذكري
يا مسيل الخير والخصب الثرى
أنت يا أرض اللآلي والزمرّد
منبع الفيروز يجري في مياه الأنهر
حيث تهوى درر الأقمار ليلاً تتبرر
أنت يا منجم برّ أصفر
أنت يا شلال ماس في الصباح النيّر
فاذكري
انه الياقوت أغلى جوهرك
واذكري
أنّ عصر البعث أسمى اعصرك
فيه آلاف العيون النيّرات
فقدت في لمحة ومض الحياة
فيه آلاف الأيادي الخيّرات
وهبتك الخير اذ جمّدها ثلج الممات
واذكري
أن نهر الدم أغنى أنهرك
سال من أعراق أبنائك ، جيل التضحيات

206

Salmā al-Khaḍrā al-Jayyūsī

Elegy to the Martyrs

I know that they died "so the homeland might live,"
Our homeland, the land of the murdered, a field soaked in blood;
I know that freedom is red, and this its price,
Its awesome price, all drenched in sighs;
I know . . . but the sorrow in my heart's depths knows not.
I weep for every eye that lost the light of life,
For every soul that breathed its last.

Remember,
O stream of abundant and fertile wealth,
O land of emerald and pearl,
Where mines of turquoise flow in riverbeds,
And pearls of moonlight bathe in the cool of night,
O hoard of yellow golddust,
O waterfall of diamonds in the morning light,
Remember—
The ruby is your most precious jewel,
And remember—
The season of rebirth is your proudest time,
With its thousands of bright springs
That once lost, in an instant, the sheen of life,
Its thousands of generous hands,
And your bounteous gift, once frozen by the snow of death,
And remember—
The river of blood is your most precious river,
It flowed from the veins of your sons—generations of sacrifice—

في ثراك الخيّر المعطار ذابوا واضمحلّوا
بعد ما كانوا يفيضون حياة أين حلّوا
كان كل منهم يختال في عرض الطريق
بالشباب الغضّ ، بالآمال خضرا ، بالأماني
بعضهم لاهٍ عن الدنيا وبعض يتلهى بهواها
وفريق يزرعُ الخيرات فيها وفريق
يقطف الخيرات والأزهار منها والأغاني
كان بعض منهم يختال في جنى كماها
بقوى الانسان .. كانوا بشرا كالآخرين
بشرا في ضعفهم ، في عزمهم ، في مبتغاهم
في أفانين الأماني وتباريح الحنين .
ثم ... لمّا صدمت اسطورة الشر رؤاهم
وتحدّاهم سؤال راعف الأصداء ثائر
« أهو الحق وموت الشر ، أم وأد الطموح
أخنوع وحياة ... أم إباء وجموح ؟
عقدوا عزمهم ... فامتلأت بيض المقابر
بالشباب الغض ، بالآمال الخضرا ، والعطور
بالحياة الحرّة المعطاء فاضت من أخاديد القبور

* * *

هكذا ماتوا ، ويمضي غيرهم نحو المصير
قدر محتومة رؤياه يا جيل العطاء !
رعشة محمومة تجتاح قلبي وتثير
دمعة الحزن بعينيّ وومض الكبرياء

And into your kind, sweet-scented soil they vanished and dis-
solved
Who once dispensed life wherever they went.
Each would go drunk along his way
With fresh youth, with verdant hope, with desire,
Some oblivious of the world, others infatuated with its love,
Some planting the seeds of good,
Others reaping, with flower and song,
And some scheming to pluck the red lips' fruit . . .
They were men like others,
In their weakness and resolve, in their longing,
In manifold hope, in painful yearning,
Then . . . when the legend of evil shattered their dream,
And a question challenged them, with its echo, abrupt and harsh:
"Shall it be justice and evil's death, or ambition buried alive?
A life in submission, or obstinate refusal?"
They formed their resolve, and the empty tombs
Were filled
With fresh youth, with verdant hope, with desire
With a free life freely given,
Overflowing from the grave's dark pit.

Thus did they die, and others yet follow on their path,
Their dream a fate ineluctable, generation of sacrifice!
A feverish shudder floods my heart, and to my eye comes
A tear of sorrow, and a flash of pride.

توفيق صايغ

فزع

طفلان ، أنت وأنا :
نبكي ، نطلبُ دميةً ،
فان تجىءْ مزركشةً لنا ،
رميناها ولمْ نلعبْ ،
وعمَّ الصراخُ الدُّنى .
طفلان
طفلان ، أنت وأنا .
عرَفتَ ما تبغينَ ، وعرفت ،
فهويْتَ في المسعي ، وهويْتُ؛
وحدّقتَ في عيني ، وحدّقتُ ،
فأسبلتُهما ، وأسبلتُ .
مَيْتةً ومَيْتُ .
عطشنا ، فرُحْنا إلى النبع فوق الجبالِ ،
ولم نخشَ أُسْداً وسطَ أدغال .
... وفي النبع لمحْنا خيالكَ وخيالي ؛
فاستدرْنا ، وماتتْ على شفاهي « تعالى » .

على السفح قبضْتِ على يدٍ من حديدِ ،
وأشحتُما عنْ تائهَ وحيدِ .
يلمسُ الصدرَ ، فيلُفّيه من جليدٍ ،
وألمس صدري ، فألْفيه مِن جليدٍ ؛
ولمْ أردْ ، ولمْ تُريدي .

القصيدة ٢٢

إلى أن انزاحَ الستارُ الأخير
كان في حبّنا نقصٌ

210

Tawfīq Ṣāyigh

Alarm

Two children, you and I:
We cry, asking for a doll,
but if one should come to us, adorned,
we would fling it away, and not play,
and our crying would prevail.
Two children
Two children, you and I.

You knew what you wanted, and I knew,
You failed in the attempt, and I failed.
You gazed into my eyes, and I gazed
You cast down your eyes, and I mine:
A dead girl, and a dead man.

We were thirsty, and went to the spring on the mountain top,
not fearing the lion in the midst of the thicket.
In the spring we noticed your reflection, my reflection
We turned around: and "Come" died upon my lips

At the foot of the mountain you grasped a hand of iron
The two of you turned from a lone wanderer.
He touches the breast, and finds it made of ice
I touch my breast, and find it made of ice.

I did not wish it; nor did you.

Poem 22

Until the last veil was cast aside
There was a blemish on our love

- خفيٌّ أليم .

كتاباً كنتُ لك ، وكنت لي كتابا ،
وعلى الرفِّ ألفُ سفر ؛
وأختاً كنت لي ، وكنتُ لك أخا ،
وكلُّ مَن في الكون اخوانٌ .
فانْ غبت وإنْ غبتُ
انتفضَ الحبُّ ولمْ يعتكفْ .
ولمْ ندرِ (ألمْ ندرِ ؟)
أنْ كان في حبّنا نقصٌ
خفيّ أليم

ظَنَنّا حبَّنا الكمال
(ظَنَنّا أمْ تعامَيْنا ؟)
فقعدْنا عنده ، سقامى ،
ولمْ نلتفتْ إلى حوضٍ قريب
تَمّحي الأسقامُ فيه
ويبلغُ الحبُّ بعدَه الكمال ،
حتّى تراءى لنا الستارُ المقيت .
بـلا أرجل سعيْنا ،
بطيئاً بطيئاً زَحَفْنا ؛
هل خشينا المياه ؟
مـن مياه البعث ارتعبْنا .
(رائدَيْنِ كنّا ، أم كنّا نزورُ أوطانا ؟)
وفي الحوضِ ارتميْنا ،
إرتميْنا حتى أرتويْنا
عندما انزاحَ الستارُ الأخير .

Hidden, painful.
I was a book to you, and you to me,
And on the shelf a thousand tomes;
You were a sister to me, and a brother I to you,
And all on earth are brothers.
Should you disappear, or I,
Then Love would tremble, yet not fade away.
We did not know (did we not?)
That there was a blemish on our love,
Hidden, painful.

We supposed our love perfection
(Did we suppose, or pretend not to see?)
So indolent we remained, ailing,
Heedless of a nearby pool
In which ailments are dissolved
And afterwards love attains perfection;
Until the hateful veil was revealed to us.
Legless we proceeded,
Slowly, slowly we crept,
Did we fear the waters?
We were alarmed at the waters of resurrection.
(Were we explorers, or visiting our homelands?)
We plunged into the pool,
We immersed ourselves until we quenched our thirst

When the last veil was cast aside.

خدعتِني ، فلم أُبالِ :
لأنّكِ انتقيت
يوم بَحثتِ عن حبيبٍ
صديقي .
أحببتْه ، وقبلكِ أحببتُهُ ،
فتلاقى حبّي وحبُّكِ ؛
ويكفيني .
كان يكفيني
لو انّكِ لمْ تهدفي
أن تخنُقي صداقتي لهُ
بحبّكِ .
أن تخنُقي الصداقةَ
وتصرَعي الحبّ :
أنْ تذبَحي الفتى
على مرأى أبيه ،
وبعدَها تذبَحيه .

لمْ أُبالِ :
لأنّ حبّكِ كانَ سيخبو
اليومَ أو غدًا ،
فخبا اليومَ
واسترحتُ .

طعنتِني ، فلم أقضِ ،
والتفتُّ ، فاذا أنت التي تُلْحَدين .
وعلى رمسكِ خططتُ :
« فلتمتْ حبيبتي ، وليعشْ صديقي » .

Poem 23

You deceived me, yet I minded not:
For you chose
That day you sought a lover
My friend.
You loved him, and I loved him before,
So my love merged with yours;
And I am content.
I would have been content
Had you not designed
To stifle my affection for him
With your love,
To stifle affection
And dash Love against the ground:
To immolate the youth
Before his father's eyes,
And then to slay the father.

I minded not:
For your love would have expired
Tomorrow or today,
And it died today
And I found peace.

You thrust at me, yet I did not die,
I turned and Lo! It is you they are interring.
I inscribed upon your tomb:
"May my beloved die, and my friend live."

ثم ماذا

ثُمَّ ماذا ؟
يقلبُ الملهاةَ مأساةً
يمحو عن المأساةِ الجلالَ
مردادٌ خفيت
يُبْبُبْغي :
ثُمَّ ماذا ؟

دُنايَ الفراغ ،
أوكارٌ حبالى
بـ ثمَّ ماذا ؟
إنْ يعتكفْ يوماً
وتمتلي وجناتُ الدُّنى
يسلُّ اللونَ منها
فزعٌ يومض
ورعدٌ يقحّ :
ثم ماذا ؟

مَصيفي الفراغُ ،
مَشْتايَ الفزع ؛
وعَيْشِي قطارٌ بينهُما
صفيره
ثمَّ ماذا ؟

مع َقهوةِ الصباح
ثمَّ ماذا ؟
وطوالَ ساعاتِ العمل
ثمَّ ماذا ؟
وقبالةَ الأوراق
وبينَ طيّاتِ الفَراش
ثمَّ ماذا ؟

216

And Then?

And then?
The question makes a tragedy out of a comedy
Robs the tragedy of its pomp
Muffled, persistent
Squawks out
And then?

My world is a void
Caverns pregnant with the question
And then?
If one day it retreats
And the cheeks of the world are suffused
The color is drained from them
By fear flashing forth
And thunder coughing out
And then?

I spend my summers in emptiness
My winters in horror
My life a train passing between them
Whistling
And then?

With my morning coffee
And then?
Throughout the hours of work
And then?
In front of the blank pages
In the folds of the sheets on the bed
And then?

وكَما هُنا هُناكَ
ثمّ ماذا ؟

يَقُضُ اليومَ
ثمّ ماذا ؟
ولا يُبْقِي منهُ رسماً لغَدٍ ،
ويَحنُو على أطلال أمسٍ
كانتْ دياراً وبُستانَا
لولا
ثمّ ماذا ؟

وفي
ثمّ ماذا ؟
مَغْمَسْتُ أيّامي .

الموعظة على الجبل

أنا أيضاً اتّبعتُهُ ،
غذّيتُ قوّتَهُ بضعفي ،
وأعنتُهُ على تحقيق ذاتِه .

على التلّة اللثغاء
التي انتظرَها طويلاً ذراعانِ مُتراخيانِ
لبحيرتِنا النعسة
(كدمعةٍ يتشوّق اليها الخدُّ
وتقربطُّ بعينْ) ،
اكلتُ مع الآكلين ،
ورأيتهم يُهلّلون لهُ ، وقد شبعوا ،
ويتدحرجون في اثره .
وحدي لبثتُ على التلّة ،
وراقبتُهُ يستمعُ للمياه تعلنُ الولاءَ بصمت
ومختاروه مِن حوله يُقَوقِئون .
وحدي لبثتُ ، أنتظرُ عودتَه .

218

Here as there
And then?

It devours the day
And then?
Leaves of it no trace for the morrow
Takes pity on the ruins of yesterday
Which would have been dwellings and gardens
But for
And then

In asking
And then
I have squandered the days of my life.

The Sermon on the Mount

I too followed him,
married my frailty to his virtue, and
helped him reveal himself.

On the lisping hill, long waited for
by the dull arms of drowsy Kinnereth
(like a couple of tears the cheeks expect,
that cling to feeble eyes), I shared the meal
of the thick-necked multitude. Well-fed,
they hailed him Lord and rolled down after him.
Alone I lay upon the hill, watched him
accept the silent homage of water
amid the crow-like shrieks of his elect.
Alone I lay, waiting for his return.

عرفتُ أنَّهُ سيعود :
فالأرغفةُ الباردة وقطعُ السمك
(ولو انَّ يديْ أمّ لفّتاها
ولو انّها ببركة أمِّ تملّحتْ)
تركتْني أتضوّرُ جوعاً .
والمياه الّتي انقلبتْ خموراً
عادتْ مياهاً على شفتيّ .
والوحلُ الذي نقّى من الوحل عينيْ برتماوسَ
جعلَ عينيَّ تسأمان ما كانتا تتنزّهان به .
والنداءُ الذي أعادَ فتى نايين للحياة
تركَ أمّي في سَواد .
على تلّة الْحصب
وسطَ السنابل تتعالى كشموعٍ
وتتلوّنُ خدودها إذْ يغمزُها
بعيون متعبة
سمكٌ لا ينامٍ ،
تضوّرتُ جوعاً .
أنا جُرِّبْتُ أيضاً :
في غيرِ بَرِّيَّةٍ جُرِّبْت .
وعاد .
مـن المياه تنبع ُ آلهةُ الحبْ .
عادَ ، وفتحَ فاه
(وقالَ قومٌ انّهُ تغنّى
وقالَ قومٌ انّها صلاة) ؛
هل سمعَهُ سواي ؟ ظننتُ
أنّهُ كانَ يُسَرُّ لي .
لمْ يناديني ، وخرجتُ ؛
ولمْ يكسّرْ أرغفةً ولمْ يلمسْ دنانا ،
وامتلأت السلالُ مـن جديد
ورأيتُ المعازيم الذين اضاعوا الوعي بوعيٍ يتلمّظون ؛

220

I knew he would return.
Cold crumbs and fish (though by a mother's hands
wrapped and with a mother's blessings salted)
left me starved. Water-turned-to-wine
tasted water to my lips. The mud
that cleared Bartimeus' eyes of mud, made mine
unsatisfied with what they feasted on.
The call that once restored to life the lad
of Nain, left my mother in black. Upon
the fertile hill, and the candle-like
corn, by the lake, wherein the sleepless fish
make weary passes at the blushing corn,
I starved.
I too was tempted, in no wilderness.

And he came.
Divinities of love spring out of sea.
He came and talked (some say he prayed, and some
he sang). Did others hear? I thought he talked
only to me. He called me not, and I
came forth. He broke no loaves, and touched no jars,
baskets were full again; the wedding-guests,
unconscious, conscious sipped the better wine.

ولمْ يبصقْ على الارض المتجدّدة ،
واذا سبعةُ المجدل سبعونَ ؛
اذْ فتحَ فاه .

على التلّة أضْطَجِـعِ .
وحينَ تُعَرِّجُ عليها الشمسُ
فتزيد حرارتَها
ولا تزيدُ الضياء ،
أهُبُّ لملاقاة الموجة
التي تجيئُني بغيرِ مِجَذاف .
في موطني ، إلى موطني أحجّ .

وأعرفُ أنّهُ سيعود .
وأنتظرُ عودتَه
(مقبرتُنا الآنَ على التلّة) .
اليها سيعودُ ، مخلِّفاً الجموعَ ،
ليبحثَ عنْ مسندِ رأس .
وقدْ يفتحُ فاه
وقد أسمعُ « طوبَى — » .

جبرا ابراهيم جبرا

من متوالية شعرية

بصوتي أتكلم .
وان هدرتُ فالبحر كان رفيقي ،
ومن عاشر القوم أربعين يوماً —
ولكنني عاشرته أربعين عاماً ،
وقذفتني كلّ فجر ، مثله ،
على الشطآن العارية .

He spat not on the brown converted ground,
I saw the tempters join the seven from
adjacent Magdala. He only talked.

On the hill I lie. And when the sun
steps in, increases then the heat but not
the light, I go to meet the oarless wave.
I am a pilgrim in my native land.

I know he will return, and wait for him
(the cemetery now stands upon the hill).
Thither, leaving all, he would repair,
as he was wont, to seek the fox's lair
and pray. Haply he may repeat:

> "Blessed are . . ."

Jabrā Ibrāhīm Jabrā

From a Poem Sequence
X

I speak in my own voice;
If I sometimes roar it's because I've had the sea for friend,
And he who accompanies someone for forty days—
But I have accompanied it for forty years,
And like it flung myself at every dawn
Upon the long bare beaches.

بصوتي اتكلم من خلال قناع الحديد
والصَّخَر ، وكلُّ لفظة مني
مركبٌ يقلعُ فيه الفُ مغامر .
بين القطيع وقفت هنا
على رجليَّ بين القو اثم السائمة
ورأسي يضرب الشمس بلا تردد :
أيةُ خرافة هذه التي تريدني
ان امرّغ الرَّأس بين إليَتَيْ كلِّ ذي أربع ؟
هنا وقفت لكيما
اصنعَ الاسطورةَ والحقيقةَ على نهجي
واعيش عنف حُلمي والحقيقة .
وحُلمي أشدُّ وعياً
أشدُّ عضّاً في الجسد
(كالبحر) من كل حقيقة .

في بوادي النفي

في بوادي النفي ربيعاً تلو ربيعْ
ما الذي فاعلون نحن جبنا
وملء عيوننا الآن ترابٌ وصقيع ؟

أرضُنا فلسطينُ خضراؤنا ،
كالرسم على بُرُد النساء ازهارُها ،
آذارُها يرصع الرواني
شقائقاً ونرجساً ،
نيسانها يُفجّر السهولَ
نوّاراً وعرائساً ،
أيارُها موّالنا
نغنيه ظهراً في الظلال الزرق
بين زيتون الوهاد ،

I speak in my own voice through a mask
Of iron and stone, but every word of mine
Is a ship in which a thousand adventurers may sail.
Amid the flocks I stand,
Firm-footed among the aimless hoofs,
My head hitting the sun unhesitatingly:
What nonsense is this that says I should
Shove my face into the backside of everyone four-limbed?
Here I stand and make
Both myth and reality in my own way
And live the violence of my dream and reality.
My dream is even more awake
More biting into the flesh
(Like the sea) than all reality.

In The Deserts of Exile

Spring after spring,
In the deserts of exile,
What are we doing with our love,
When our eyes are full of frost and dust?

Our Palestine, green land of ours;
Its flowers as if embroidered of women's gowns;
March adorns its hills
With the jewel-like peony and narcissus;
April bursts open in its plains
With flowers and bride-like blossoms;
May is our rustic song
Which we sing at noon,
In the blue shadows,
Among the olive-trees of our valleys,

نترقب في نضج الحقول وفاء تموزَ
ورقصةَ الدبكة في الحصاد .

آيْ أرضَنا ، حيث صبانا قد تقضّى
حُلْماً في ظلال البرتقال ،
بين لوزات الوهاد —
اذكرينا الآن مطوّفين
بين اشواك القفار
مطوّفين في صمّ الجبال
اذكرينا الآن في
هوج المدائن عبر البوادي والبحار ،
اذكرينا وملء الاعين منا
غبار لا ينجلي من سرعة الحلّ والرحال .
سحقوا زهر الروابي حولنا
هدموا الدور علينا
بعثروا الاشلاء منا
بسطوا الفلاة أمامنا
واذا الوهاد بحشاها تتلوى
والظلال الزرق تتصدع شوكاً
احمرَ ينحني
على جثثٍ بقيَتْ نهبَ العُقابِ والغراب .

أمن ذراك غنت الملائكُ للرعاة
أنشودة السلام والمسرَّة للبشر !
لم يضحك سوى الموْت اذ رأى
بين امعاء الدواب
اضلعَ البشر ،
وخلالَ قهقهة الرصاص
راح يرقص دبكةً
على رؤوس الباكيات

226

And in the ripeness of the fields
We wait for the promise of July
And the joyous dance amidst the harvest.

O land of ours where our childhood passed
Like dreams in the shade of the orange-grove,
Among the almond-trees in the valleys—
Remember us now wandering
Among the thorns of the desert,
Wandering in rocky mountains;
Remember us now
In the tumult of cities beyond deserts and seas;
Remember us
With our eyes full of dust
That never clears in our ceaseless wandering.
They crushed the flowers on the hills around us,
Destroyed the houses over our heads,
Scattered our torn remains,
Then unfolded the desert before us,
With valleys writhing in hunger
And blue shadows shattered into red thorns
Bent over corpses left as prey for falcon and crow.

Is it from your hills that the angels sang to the shepherds
Of peace on earth and goodwill among men?
Only death laughed when it saw
Among the entrails of beasts
The ribs of men,
And through the guffaw of bullets
It went dancing a joyous dance
On the heads of weeping women.

زمرّدٌ أرضُنا —
ولكن في بوادي النفيِ
ربيعاً تلو ربيعْ
لا يفحّ الا النقيعُ في وجهنا .
ما الذي ، ما الذي فاعلون نحن بحبنا
وملء عيوننا ، افواهنا ، الآن ترابٌ وصقيع

محمود درويش

جبين وغضب

وطني ! يا ايها النسرُ
الذي يُغمد منقار اللهبْ
في عيوني
عبر قضبان الخشب .
كلُّ ما أملكه في حضرة الموت :
جبين وغضب .
وأنا أوصيتُ ان يزرع قلبي شجره
وجبيني منزلاً للقُبرَّه .
أيها النسر الذي
لستُ جديراً بجناحكْ
انني أوثر اكليل اللهب .
وطني ، انّا وُلدنا وكبرنا بجراحك
وأكلنا شجر البلّوط ..
كي نشهد ميلاد صباحك
أيها النسر الذي يرسف في الاغلال
من دون سبب
أيها الموت الخرافيّ الذي كان بـيحبّ ..
لم يزل منقارك الاحمر في عيي

Our land is an emerald,
But in the deserts of exile,
Spring after spring,
Only the dust hisses in our face.
What then, what are we doing with our love?
When our eyes and our mouth are full of frost and dust?

Maḥmūd Darwīsh

Pride and Fury

O homeland! O eagle,
Plunging, through the bars of my cell,
Your fiery beak in my eyes!
All I possess in the presence of death
Is pride and fury.
I have willed that my heart be planted as a tree,
That my forehead become an abode for skylarks.
O eagle,
I am unworthy of your lofty wing,
I prefer a crown of flame.
O homeland!
We were born and raised in your wound,
And ate the fruit of your trees,
To witness the birth of your daybreak.
O eagle unjustly languishing in chains,
O legendary death which once was sought,
Your fiery beak is still plunged in my eye,

سيفاً من لهب ..
وأنا لستُ جديراً بجناحك
كلُّ ما أملكه في حضرة الموت :
جبين .. وغضب ! .

هارون هاشم رشيد

فلسطيني

فلسطيني ..
أنا اسمي .. فلسطيني
نقشت اسمي
على كل الميادين
بخط بارز يسمو
على كل العناوين
حروف اسمى تلاصقني
تعايشني .. تغذيني
تبث النار في روحي
وتنبض في شرابيني
هو اسمى .. انني أدري
يعذبني .. ويشقيني
تطاردني عيونهم
لأن اسمي فلسطيني
تطاردني .. تلاحقني
تتابعني .. وتؤذيني
لأن اسمي فلسطيني
كما شاءوا أضاعوني
أنا عشت الذي قد عشت
مجهول التلاوين
بما شاءوا من الالوان
والالقاب أعطوني

Like a sword of flame.
Unworthy of your lofty wing,
All I possess in the presence of death
Is pride and fury.

Hārūn Hāshim Rashīd

Palestinian

Palestinian,
Palestinian is my name.
In a clear script,
On all battlefields,
I have inscribed my name,
Eclipsing all other titles.
The letters of my name cling to me,
Live with me, nourish me,
Fill my soul with fire
And pulse through my veins.
Palestinian,
Such is my name, I know.
It torments and grieves me,
Their eyes hunt me,
Pursue me, wound me.
For my name is Palestinian
And as they pleased
They have made me wander.

I have lived all my life
Without traits and features,
And as they pleased,
They gave me names and titles.

وأبواب السجون على
مصارعها تناديني
وفي كل مطارات الدني
اسمي .. عناويني
رياح الافك تحملني
وتنشرني .. وتطويني
فلسطيني تلاحقني
تعيش معي فلسطيني
فلسطيني وذا قدري
يلازمني .. ويحييني
فلسطيني وان داسوا
على اسمي وداسوني
فلسطيني وان خانوا
تعاليمي وخانوني
فلسطيني ولو أنهمو
في السوق باعوني
كما شاءوا .. بما شاءوا
بآلاف الملايين
فلسطيني ولو حتى
إلى الاعواد ساقوني
فلسطيني ولو حتى
إلى الجدران شدوني
فلسطيني .. فلسطيني
ولو للنار زفوني
أنا .. ماذا أكون أنا
بلا اسمي فلسطيني
بلا وطن أعيش له
وأحميه ويحميني
أنا ماذا أكون أنا
أجيبوني .. أجيبوني

Jails with their gates flung wide
Summon me,
And in all the airports of the world
Are found my names and titles—
The lying wind carries me,
Disperses me.
Palestinian—
The name pursues me, lives with me;
Palestinian is my fate,
Clinging to me, reviving me.
Palestinian I am,
Though they trample me and my name;
Palestinian I am,
Though they betray me and my cause;
Palestinian I am,
Though they sell me in the market
For what they please,
For thousands of millions;
Palestinian I am,
Though to the gallows they drive me;
Palestinian I am,
Though to the walls they bind me.
Palestinian I am,
Palestinian I am,
Though to the flames they cast me.
I—what am I?
Without my name, Palestinian,
Without a homeland to live for,
To protect and be protected by?
I—what am I?
Answer me, answer me!

Biographical Notes

Gibrān Khalīl Gibrān (1883–1931)

Gibrān was born on December 6, 1883, and died on April 10, 1931. He studied in Lebanon but spent most of his life in America. He wrote prolifically in Arabic and English and distinguished himself in the Western world as a painter and sculptor. Gibrān was one of the first writers to use "free verse" effectively in Arabic poetry; and in his revolt against traditional formalism he broke new ground and greatly influenced succeeding generations of Arab poets and writers. "Two Voices" is taken from his *al-Mawākib* (The Processions).

Amīn al-Rīḥānī (1876–1940)

Born in the Lebanese village of Frayka in 1876, al-Rīḥānī first visited the United States when he was twelve years old. After pursuing his schooling for one year, he began working in commerce with his father and uncle. This activity was temporarily interrupted when at the age of seventeen he joined a travelling theatrical group and spent three months travelling over America. Simultaneously he studied at a night school in New York, reading deeply in Western literature, and trying to set down his thoughts for the New York Arabic newspaper *al-Hudā*. In 1898 he returned to Lebanon and consolidated his command of the Arabic language. During this residence in Lebanon, he became acquainted with the Arab classics, especially the works of al-Maʿarrī including *al-Luzūmiyyāt*, selections from which he was later to translate into English. His interest in his Arab legacy led him to the idea of an extended journey through the Arab world, the impressions of which he recorded in a series of valuable travelogues. The rest of

235

his life was divided between America and the Arab world, and was occupied by a prolific literary production. His main concerns were a cultural rapprochement between East and West and the revivification of Arabic letters. In New York, together with Gibrān Khalīl Gibrān, Mīkhā'īl Nuʿaymah and other writers, he founded a literary society known as *al-Rābiṭah al-Qalamīyah* (The Pen League), which exerted great influence on the development of modern Arabic literature.

Among his major works in Arabic are *Mulūk al-ʿArab* (Arab Kings), *Qalb al-ʿIrāq* (The Heart of Iraq), and *al-Rīhāniyāt* (collected prose poems). His publications in English include *The Coasts of Arabic, A Chant of Mystics, The Book of Khalid, Myrtle and Myrrh*.

The poem translated here is taken from *al-Rīhāniyāt*, composed in a genre which al-Rīhānī helped to pioneer in modern Arabic.

Mīkhā'īl Nuʿaymah (1889–   )

Born in Lebanon in 1889, Nuʿaymah was educated in Russian Orthodox schools in his homeland and in Nazareth, Palestine. He later spent five years (1906–1911) at an ecclesiastical seminary in Poltava, Russia. In 1912 he went to the United States, and after receiving his law degree from the University of Washington in Seattle, he worked for several years in New York. There, he founded with Gibrān and other Syro-American writers *al-Rābiṭah al-Qalamīyah*, the first modernizing school of Arabic literature, and became one of the most distinguished figures among the Arab writers and intellectuals of this century. In 1932 Nuʿaymah returned to Lebanon to resume his remarkable contribution to the renaissance of Arabic letters—writing stories, novels, plays, biographies and literary criticism. The poetic selections included here are taken from his collected poems, *Hams al-Jufūn* (Eyelid Whisperings). The poems "My Brother," "Autumn Leaves" and "Peace of Mind" have been translated by Roger Monroe.

Ilīyā Abū Māḍī (1890–1957)

Born in 1890 in Lebanon, Abū Māḍī spent a few years in Egypt, then migrated to the United States in 1911. There, he collaborated with Gibrān, Nuʿaymah and other Syro-Americans in *al-Rābiṭah al-Qalamīyah* (The Pen League) and distinguished himself as a poet and journalist. He published several collections including *al-Jadāwil* (Streams), *al-Khamāʾil* (Gardens), and *Tibr wa Turāb* (Golddust and Earth). The selection, "Cryptic Charms" (*al-Ṭalāsim*), is an extract from his philosophical poem of the same title, and was translated in collaboration with Julie Meisami. It exemplifies the skepticism and nostalgia that underlie much of his work.

Fawzī al-Maʿlūf (1899–1930)

Al-Maʿlūf was born in the Lebanese town of Zaḥlah in 1899. He migrated to South America and settled in Rio de Janeiro where he died in 1930. He is best known for his epic, *ʿAlā Bisāṭ al-Rīḥ* (On the Carpet of the Wind), which appeared simultaneously in Arabic, Spanish and Portuguese in Brazil in 1930. Together with his brother, Shafīq al-Maʿlūf, editor of *Majallat al-ʿUṣbah al-Andalusīyah* (Review of the Andalusian League), Fawzī is considered the most distinguished of the Syro-American poets of the southern hemisphere. His two cantos, "King in the Air" and "Strewn Leaves," were translated in collaboration with Michael Zwettler. Nostalgia and melancholy, expressed in elegant lyrical form, are the keynotes of his poetry.

Khalīl Muṭrān (1872–1949)

Born in 1872 in Baalbek, Lebanon, Muṭrān completed his primary studies at the Elementary Oriental School in Zaḥlah. He then entered the Roman Catholic Patriarchal College in Beirut, where he was taught French by native speakers of the language. He was also trained there in Arabic disciplines by the Lebanese scholar Ibrāhīm al-Yāzijī and his brother Khalīl. As a result of his political activity against the Ottoman regime, he was obliged to take refuge in Paris, where he pursued his intellectual interests. In 1892, Muṭrān left Paris for Egypt where he lived for the rest of his life. It was during this long period, 1892 to 1949, that Muṭrān established himself as a competent journalist and as one of the most influential modernizing poets of his generation. His publications include the *Dīwān* in four volumes, from which "A Rose that Died" and "Nero" are taken.

Ilyās Abū Shabakah (1904–1947)

Born in New York in 1904, Abū Shabakah returned with his parents to Lebanon while still very young. He studied at ʿAynṭūrah College, receiving a thorough training in both Arabic and French language and literature. He died in 1947 at the age of forty-three. Abū Shabakah is considered one of the leading romanticists in modern Arabic poetry. His collected poems include *Afāʿi al-Firdaws* (Serpents of Paradise), *al-Alḥān* (The Songs), *Ghalwā'* (Olga), *Ilā al-Abad* (Unto Eternity), *Min Saʿīd al-Ālihah* (From the Uplands of the Gods) and *Nidā al-Qalb* (Call of the Heart). He also made numerous translations from French classical and romantic literature.

Albert Adīb (1908–   )

Born in Mexico, Adīb lived and studied in Egypt for several years. He later moved to Lebanon. In 1942 he founded *al-Adīb* review which became a remarkable forum for the new generation of Arab poets and writers. Adīb is one of the pioneers of the free verse movement and his poem "Fidelity" reflects his experimentation with this new poetic form.

Saʿīd ʿAql (1912–   )

Born in 1912 in Zaḥlah, Lebanon, ʿAql is one of Lebanon's foremost poets. His poetical production, first as a romanticist and later as a symbolist, greatly influenced the new generation of poets who made a violent breach with the antiquated esthetics of classical Arabic poetry. His works include *Bint Yāftah* (The Daughter of Jafta), *Qudmūs*, *al-Majdalīyah* (The Magdalen), *Rindalah*, *Ajmal minki? Lā!* (More Beautiful Than You? No!), *Lubnān in Ḥakā* (Should Lebanon Speak), and *Ka's li-Khamr* (A Winecup).

Ṣalāḥ Labakī (1906–1955)

Born in Brazil in 1906, Labakī came to Lebanon in 1908. He studied at the Ḥikmah College in Beirut and at ʿAynṭūrah. He founded the Lebanese literary society, *Ahl al-Qalam,* and became a leading symbolist poet. He has published *Ḥanīn* (Longing), *Mawāᶜid* (Rendezvous), *Sa'am* (Boredom), *Urjūḥat al-Qamar* (The Swing of the Moon) and *Ghurabā* (Strangers).

Yūsuf al-Khāl (1917–   )

Al-Khāl was born in Tripoli, Lebanon in 1917; he studied at the American University in Beirut where he has also taught for a few years. In 1947, he became editor of *Ṣawt al-Mar'ah* (The Voice of Woman). In 1948, his journalistic career brought him to New York where he worked for the United Nations Secretariat until 1952; he then edited the newspaper *al-Hudā* until his return to Lebanon in 1955. Two years later, he founded and edited *Majallat Shiᶜr* (Poetry Review), which became the most influential forum for the free verse movement in Arabic poetry. Currently al-Khāl is one of the editors of *Dār al-Nahār* publishing house in Beirut. His own publications include *al-Bi'r al-Mahjūrah* (The Abandoned Well), *al-Hurriyyah* (Freedom), *Qaṣā'id fī al-Arbaᶜīn* (Poems at Forty), *Qaṣā'id Mukhtārah* (Selected Poems) and *Hirūdiyah* (Herodias). He has also made translations of the works of T. S. Eliot, Ezra Pound, Robert Frost and others.

Khalīl Hāwī (1925–   )

Born in 1925 in Shuwair, Lebanon, Hāwī was educated at the American University in Beirut and then at Cambridge University, England, where he wrote his dissertation on Gibrān. He is presently Professor of Arabic Literature at the American University in Beirut and a highly regarded poet. His publications include *Bayādir al-Jūᶜ* (Threshing Floors of Hunger), *Nahr al-Ramād* (River of Ashes), and *al-Nay wa al-Rīh* (The Flute and the Wind). His work is characterized by its marked intellectual and social content.

Unsī al-Ḥājj (1937–   )

Al-Ḥājj was born in Beirut in 1937, and started his literary career as a journalist working for the daily *al-Nahār*. He was soon recognized as an outstanding poet-critic. Greatly influenced by modern French literature, he has made several translations, particularly of the works of Prévert, Breton and Artaud. He is an active participant in the literary movement led by *Majallat Shiʿr*, and is at present the literary and artistic director of *al-Nahār*. His collections include *Lan* (Never), *al-Ra's al-Maqṭūʿ* (The Severed Head) and *Māḍī al-Ayyām al-Ātiyah* (The Past of the Coming Days). His poetry displays surrealistic tendencies and a violent dislocation of conventional poetic idiom.

Aḥmad al-Ṣāfī al-Najafī (1894–   )

Born in Najaf, Iraq, in 1894, al-Najafī spent several years of his youth in southern Iran where he studied Persian and translated the *Rubāʿiyat* of ʿUmar Khayyām into Arabic. He left Iraq for Lebanon where he currently resides. Though a neo-classicist, al-Najafī shows little concern for formal perfection and reveals instead serious preoccupation with the content of his poetry. Among his works are *al-Aghwār* (The Depths), *Alḥān al-Lahīb* (Songs of Fire), *al-Amwāj* (The Waves), *Ḥiṣād al-Sijn* (The Harvest of Prison) and *al-Shallāl* (The Falls).

Nāzik al-Malāʾikah (1923–   )

Born in Baghdad in 1923, al-Malāʾikah studied Arabic literature at Baghdad University and later attended Princeton, where she made an extensive study of English literature. Upon her return to Iraq, she assumed a leading role in the free verse movement, both through her own compositions and through her important critical work. She has published numerous collections including *ʿĀshiqat al-Layl* (Lover of the Night), *Shaẓāyā wa Ramād* (Splinters and Ashes), *Qarārat al-Mawjah* (The Bottom of the Wave) and *Shajarat al-Qamar* (The Moon-tree).

Badr Shākir al-Sayyāb (1927–1964)

Al-Sayyāb was born in 1927 in the village of Jaikur near Basra, Iraq. He was educated first in Basra, and then at the Teachers' College in Baghdad, where he studied Arabic and English literature. He briefly worked as a teacher before passing into political activity. His poetry mirrored the contending political currents in the Arab world, and although his affiliations changed more than once, his abiding concern was the effective poetic expression of his loyalties. He died at a tragically early age in London in 1964 while undergoing treatment for a serious illness. He must be regarded as one of the pioneers of the free verse movement and is, without doubt, the greatest of the contemporary Arab poets. His poetical collections include *Awrāq Dhābilah* (Fading Leaves), *Azhār wa Asāṭīr* (Flowers and Legends), *al-Maʿbad al-Gharīq* (The Submerged Temple), *Iqbāl wa Shanāshīl ibnat al-Shalabī* (Iqbal and the Fancy Window of Shalabi's Daughter), *Manzil al-Aqnān* (House of the Slaves) and *Unshūdat al-Maṭar* (Songs of the Rain).

ʿAbd al-Wahhāb al-Bayātī (1926–)

Al-Bayātī was born in Baghdad in 1926, and studied at the Baghdad Teachers' College. Initially a teacher, he later turned to journalism, expressing his opposition to the royalist regime in Iraq and expounding his communist views which have caused him to spend most of his life in exile. He has lived in Lebanon, Syria, Egypt, Austria and the Soviet Union. After the overthrow of the monarchy in 1958, he was appointed by the revolutionary regime as cultural attaché at the Iraqi embassy in Moscow, a post from which he later resigned in order to teach at the Afro-Asian People's University in Moscow. Al-Bayātī is regarded as the foremost representative of the socialist realist school in modern Arabic poetry. Among his works are the following: *Abārīq Muhashshamah* (Broken Jars), *Malāʾikah wa Shayāṭīn* (Angels and Devils), *Ashʿār fī al-Manfā* (Poems in Exile), *ʿIshrūn Qaṣīdah min Barlīn* (Twenty Poems from Berlin), *Kalimāt lā Tamūt* (*Words which Do Not Die*), *al-Ladhī yaʾtī wa lā yaʾtī* (Things Which Happen and Do Not Happen), *al-Majd li al-Aṭfāl wa al-Zaytūn* (Glory to Little Children and Olives), *al-Mawt fī al-Ḥayāh* (Death in Life) and *Sifr al-Faqr wa al-Thawrah* (The Book of Poverty and Revolution).

Buland al-Ḥaydarī (1926–)

Al-Ḥaydarī was born in Iraq in 1926 of a Kurdish family. As a political activist, he was obliged to go into exile and is now living in Lebanon, where he edits the journal *al-ʿUlūm*. His poetry is inspired both by personal experience and by social conscience. His collections include *Aghānī al-Madīnah al-Maytah* (Songs of the Dead City), *Khuṭuwāt fī al-Ghurbah* (Footsteps in a Strange Land) and *Riḥlat al-Ḥurūf al-Ṣufr* (Journey of the Yellow Letters).

ʿAbd al-Raḥmān Shukrī (1886–1958)

Shukrī was born in Port Said, Egypt, in 1886. He received his secondary education in Alexandria and later studied at the Teachers' College in Cairo, graduating in 1909. After several years of study in England, he returned to Egypt. Together with al-ʿAqqād and al-Māzinī, he formed the *Dīwān* group, a modernizing movement which reinforced its counterpart in North America led by Gibrān and his Syro-American colleagues. He has published numerous collections which appeared recently in one volume entitled *Dīwān ʿAbd al-Raḥmān Shukrī*. He died in 1958.

ʿAlī Maḥmud Ṭāhā (1902–1949)

Ṭāhā was born in al-Manṣūrah, Egypt. Although by profession an engineer, he established himself as a member of the Apollo group and a leading romanticist among contemporary Arab poets. He travelled extensively in Europe and recorded his impressions in lyric poems, some of which were put to music and attained great popularity. His collections include *al-Mallāḥ al-Tā'ih* (The Errant Sailor), *Layālī al-Mallāḥ al-Tā'ih* (Nights of the Errant Sailor) and *Zahr wa Khamr* (Flowers and Wine).

Lewis ʿAwaḍ (1915–   )

Born in Egypt in 1915, ʿAwaḍ studied at Fuad I, Cambridge and Princeton Universities. He is the author of *Plutoland, Studies in Contemporary Arabic Literature* and several other critical works. He is at present cultural adviser and literary editor of the newspaper *al-Ahrām*. His poem "Kiriyalayson" is one of the earliest experiments in Arabic free verse. His "Love at St. Lazare" reveals laborious intellectual sophistication.

242

Abū al-Qāsim al-Shābbī (1909–1934)

Born in southern Tunisia in 1909, al-Shābbī studied at Zaytū-nah University and at the School of Law in Tunis. During his formative years, he was influenced by the romanticism of the Syro-American poets, a trend which he championed as a leading member of the Apollo group of poets. His poems, first published in the *Apollo* journal, were later collected under the title *Aghānī al-Ḥayāh* (Songs of Life). He died at the age of twenty-five. He is considered the most brilliant modern Arab poet of North Africa.

Ṣalāḥ ʿAbd al-Ṣabūr (1931–   )

Born in Egypt in 1931, al-Ṣabūr studied at Cairo University, becoming acquainted with modern Western literature with the help of Lewis ʿAwaḍ. Like ʿAwaḍ, he works on the literary supplement of *al-Ahrām*. He has published numerous works of literary criticism and several collections of poems including *al-Nās fī Bilādī* (The People of my Country), *Aqūl lakum* (I Say Unto You), *Aḥlām al-Fāris al-Qadīm* (The Dreams of the Ancient Knight) and *Aṣwāt al-ʿAṣr* (Voices of the Age), and the plays *Maʾsāt al-Ḥallāj* (The Tragedy of al-Hallaj) and *Laylā wa al-Majnūn* (Layla and Majnun). ʿAbd al-Ṣabūr is considered the chief representative of the free verse movement in Egypt, his poetry revealing both social depth and sophisticated introspection.

Aḥmad ʿAbd al-Muʿṭī Ḥijāzī (1935–   )

Ḥijāzī was born in a village in the Nile Delta in 1935. He studied at the Teachers' College in Cairo, and developed militant socialist tendencies which are reflected in his poetry. He has published *Madīnah bilā Qalb* (City Without a Heart), *Lam Yabqa illā al-Iʿtirāf* (Nothing Remains but Confession) and *Urās* (Horace).

Muḥammad al-Faytūrī (1930–   )

Born in 1930 of a Sudanese father and an Egyptian mother, al-Faytūrī has spent most of his life in Alexandria. He is dedicated to the liberation of the African peoples. His works are *Aghānī*

Ifrīqiyah (The Songs of Africa) and *ʿĀshiq min Ifrīqiyah* (A Lover from Africa).

ʿUmar Abū Rīshah (1910–   )

Born in Aleppo in 1908, Abū Rīsha studied at the American University in Beirut and later in England, where he acquainted himself with Western literary currents and especially with the English Romantics. On his return to Syria, he was appointed director of the National Library in Aleppo; he later joined the diplomatic service, serving as Syrian cultural attaché with the Arab League and then as ambassador to Brazil and India. His chief poetical production is the collection *Shiʿr* published in 1947, which is characterized by formal elegance and a refined sensibility. The two poems included here are taken from this collection; the second of them was translated in collaboration with Julie Meisami.

Nizār Qabbānī (1923–   )

Qabbānī was born in Damascus in 1923; he studied law and then joined the diplomatic service, being posted to Beirut, Cairo, London, Peking and Madrid. He resigned in order to establish his own publishing house in Beirut. He has published several collections. Although love was the dominant theme of his early work, he has more recently turned to political and social concerns, expressing these in a direct and effective form of free verse. His works include *Ḥabībatī* (My Beloved), *Qālat lī al-Samrāʾ* (The Dark Girl Told Me), *Qaṣāʾid* (Poems), *Samba* (Samba), *Ṭufūlat Nahd* (Childhood of a Breast), *Anti Lī* (You are Mine) and *Fatḥ* (The Palestinian Commandos).

ʿAlī Aḥmad Saʿīd (Adonis) (1930–   )

Born in Syria in 1930, Adonis attended secondary school in Tartus and Lattakia and later graduated from the Syrian University in Damascus. He began writing poetry in the early 1950's, dealing initially with themes of political inspiration. In 1956 he left Syria for political reasons and settled in Lebanon. The following year he cooperated with Yūsuf al-Khāl in editing *Majallat Shi'r* (The Poetry Review). Hs is currently publishing his own journal *Mawāqif* (Attitudes). His works include *Qālat al-Arḍ* (The Earth Said), *Qaṣā'id Ūlā* (Early Poems), *Aghānī Mihyār al-Dimashqī* (Songs of Mihyar the Damascene), *Awrāq fī al-Rīḥ* (Leaves in the Wind), *Kitāb al-Taḥawwulāt wa al-Hijrah fī Aqālīm al-Layl wa al-Nahār* (The Book of Changes and Migration in the Regions of Night and Day) and *al-Masraḥ wa al-Marāyā* (The Stage and Mirrors). He has also compiled an anthology of classical Arabic poetry in two volumes. His work is noted for its extreme purity and polish of expression, and reflects both social and intellectual concerns. He is among the most influential of contemporary poets in the Arab world.

Muḥammad al-Māghūṭ (1930–   )

Born in Nablus, Palestine, Ṭūqān is, with Nāzik al-Malā'ikah of the best prose-poets of his generation. He has published two collections: *Ḥuzn fī Ḍaw' al-Qamar* (Sorrow in the Moonlight) and *Ghurfah bi Malāyīn al-Judrān* (Room with a Million Walls), both characterized by a severe and critical tone.

Fadwā Ṭūqān (1917–   )

Born in Nablus, Palestine, Ṭūqān is, with Nāzik al-Malā'ikah and her compatriot Salmā al-Jayyūsī, among the most distinguished poetesses in the Arab world. She has published several collections including *Wajadtuhā* (I Have Found It), *Waḥdī Maʿ al-Ayyām* (Alone With the Days) and *Aʿṭinā Ḥubban* (Give Us Love). These works reveal a pessimistic and rebellious spirit, influenced by the Palestinian tragedy.

Salmā al-Jayyūsī (c. 1922–   )

Born in Ṣafad, Palestine, al-Jayyūsī studied first at the Arab College in Jerusalem, then at the American University in Beirut, and finally in London, where she wrote a doctoral dissertation on modern Arabic poetry. Her poetry, centering on the Palestinian tragedy, includes *al-ʿAwdah min al-Nabʿ al-Ḥālim* (Return from the Dreamy Fountain) and *ʿArrāf al-Rīḥ* (The Soothsayer of the Wind).

Tawfīq Ṣāyigh (1923–1971)

Ṣāyigh was born in Syria, and moved with his family to Tiberias, Palestine; he studied at the Arab College in Jerusalem, at the American University in Beirut and at Harvard. He taught Arabic at Cambridge and at London University, and from 1968 until his untimely death in January 1971 was visiting lecturer in Near Eastern Languages and Comparative Literature at the University of California, Berkeley. In 1961, he founded the bimonthly review, *Ḥiwār*, which until its cessation in 1966 was a forum for original and sometimes controversial ideas. He distinguished himself among contemporary Arab poets with such works as *Thalāthūn Qaṣīdah* (Thirty Poems), *al-Qaṣīdah Kāf* (The Poem "K"), and *Muʿallaqat Tawfīq Ṣāyigh* (The Ode of Tawfīq Ṣāyigh). Of his poems included in this anthology, *The Sermon on the Mount* was originally composed in English.

Jabrā Ibrāhīm Jabrā (1919–   )

Jabrā was born in Bethlehem, Palestine, in 1919. He studied at the Arab College in Jerusalem and later at Cambridge University. He now lives in Iraq where he has established himself as a distinguished novelist, critic, painter and poet. He has published two collections of poems: *Tammūz fī al-Madīnah* (July in the City) and *al-Madār al-Mughlaq* (The Closed Circuit). The second poem included here, entitled "From a Poem Sequence," is Jabrā's own translation.

Maḥmūd Darwīsh (1942–   )

Darwīsh is a young Palestinian poet born in al-Barwa, a village to the east of Acre. Until his recent departure for Egypt, he lived in Haifa where he edited the biweekly newspaper, *al-Ittiḥād*, and voiced in his poetry the tragic predicament of the Palestinian Arab under Zionist rule. His publications include *Ākhir al-Layl* (The End of the Night), *ʿĀshiq min Filisṭīn* (A Lover from Palestine, and *Awrāq al-Zaytūn* (Olive Leaves).

Hārūn Hāshim Rashīd (ca. 1930–   )

Rashīd is among the most noted of the Palestinian poets living now under Zionist rule. He has published *Safīnat al-Ghaḍab* (The Ship of Anger), *Maʿ al-Ghurabāʾ* (With the Strangers), *ʿAwdat al-Ghurabāʾ* (The Return of the Exiles), *Ghazzah fī Khaṭṭ al-Nār* (Gaza in the Line of Fire), *Arḍ al-Thawrāt* (The Land of Revolutions) and *Ḥattā Yaʿūd Shaʿbunā* (Until Our People Return).

Bibliography

ʿAbd al-Ṣabūr, Ṣalāḥ. "Nāzik al-Malāʾikah wa-al-Shiʿr al-Ḥurr," *al-Kātib* 24 (March 1963), 114–121.

Ahmed, Jamal Mohammed. *The Intellectual Origins of Egyptian Nationalism*. London, Oxford University Press, 1960.

Anthologie de la Littérature Arabe Contemporaine, t. III: *La Poésie*. Choix, présentation, traduction et introduction par Luc Norin et Edouard Tarabay. Paris, Editions du Seuil, 1967.

al-ʿAqqād, ʿAbbās Maḥmūd. *al-Lughah al-Shāʿirah, Mazāyā al-Fann wa-al-Taʿbīr fī al-Lughah al-ʿArabīyah*. Cairo, Maktabat Ghurayyib, 1968.

Arberry, A. J. *Arabic Poetry: A Primer for Students*. Cambridge University Press, 1965.

ʿAwaḍ, Lewis, *Plutoland wa-Qaṣāʾid Ukhrā, min Shiʿr al-Khāṣṣah*. Cairo, 1947.

––––––. "Thawrat al-ʿArūḍ," in his *Dirāsāt ʿArabīyah wa-Gharbīyah*, Cairo, 1965, pp. 121–126.

ʿAyyād, Shukrī Muḥammad. *Mūsīqā al-Shiʿr al-ʿArabī, Mashrūʿ Dirāsah ʿIlmīyah*. Cairo, Dār al-Maʿrifah, 1968.

Badawī, Muṣṭafā. *An Anthology of Modern Arabic Verse* (in Arabic). Oxford University Press, 1970.

Bā Kathīr, ʿAlī Aḥmad. *Muḥāḍarāt fī al-Masraḥīyah min khilāl Tajāribī al-Khāṣṣah*. Cairo, Maʿhad al-Dirāsāt al-ʿArabīyah al-ʿĀliyah, 1958.

––––––. "Namūdhaj min al-Shiʿr al-Mursal al-Ḥurr," *al-Risālah* XIII (1945), 280–281.

Blachère, Régis. "Métrique et Prosodie Arabes à la Lumière des Publications Récentes," *Arabica* VII:3 (1960), 225–236.

al-Dasūqī, ʿAbd al-ʿAzīz. *Jamāʿat Apollo wa-Āthāruhā fī al-Shiʿr al-Ḥadīth*. Cairo, Maʿhad al-Dirāsāt al-ʿArabīyah al-ʿAliyah, 1960.

Dayf, Shawqī. "Hādir al-Shiʿr al-ʿArabī Muttaṣil bi-Mādīh," *Mihrajān al-Shiʿr al-Thānī* (1960), pp. 161–172.

————. "Ṣināʿat al-Shiʿr al-Miṣrī fī al-Qarn al-Māḍī,"*Jāmiʿat al-Qāhirah, Majallat Kullīyat al-Ādāb* XIV:2 (1952), 37–64.

al-Dujaylī, ʿAbd al-Karīm. *al-Band fī al-Ādāb al-ʿArabī*. Baghdad, 1959.

Gabrieli, Francesco. "Literary Tendencies," in G. E. von Grunebaum (ed.), *Unity and Variety in Muslim Civilization*. Chicago, University of Chicago Press, 1965, pp. 87–106.

García Gómez, Emilio. "La Poésie Lyrique Hispano-Arabe et l'Apparition de la Lyrique Romane," *Arabica* V:2 (1958), 113–144.

Gibb, H. A. R. *Studies on the Civilization of Islam*. Ed. by S. J. Shaw and W. R. Polk. London, Oxford University Press, 1962.

————. *Arabic Literature*. 2nd ed. Clarendon Press, 1963.

Gibrān, Gibrān Khalīl. *al-Majmūʿah al-Kāmilah*. Ed. by Mīkhāʿīl Nuʿaymah. Beirut, Dār Bayrūt, 1961.

von Grunebaum, G. E. "Arabic Poetics," in *Indiana University Conference on Oriental-Western Literary Relations*. Ed. by H. Franz and G. L. Anderson. Chapel Hill, University of North Carolina Studies in Comparative Literature, 1955.

Ḥasan, Muḥammad ʿAbd al-Ghanī. *al-Shiʿr al-ʿArabī fī al-Mahjar*. 2nd ed. Cairo, Maktabat al-Khānijī, 1958.

Ḥāwī, Khalīl. *Kahlīl Gibrān*. Beirut, American University, 1963.

Hourani, Albert. *Arabic Thought in the Liberal Age, 1798–1939*. London, Oxford University Press, 1962.

al-Ḥusaynī, Isḥāq Mūsā. *al-Naqd al-Adabī al-Muʿāṣir fī al-Rubʿ al-Awwal min al-Qarn al-ʿIshrīn*. Cairo. Maʿhad al-Buḥūth wa-al-Dirāsāt al-ʿArabīyah, 1967.

Ismāʿīl, ʿIzz al-Dīn. "Nāzik al-Malāʾikah: *Qaḍāyā al-Shiʿr al-Muʿāṣir*," *al-Majallah* 73 (Jan. 1963), 116–121.

ʿIzz al-Dīn, Yūsuf. *Fī al-Adab al-ʿArabī al-Ḥadīth, Buḥūth wa-Maqālāt*. Baghdad, Maktabat al-Baṣri, 1967.

Jabr, Jamīl. *Amīn al-Rīḥānī, Sīratuhu wa-Adabuh*. Sayda, 1964.

Jabrā, Jabrā Ibrāhīm. "al-Shiʿr al-Ḥurr wa-al-Naqd al-Khāṭiʾ," in his *al-Riḥlah al-Thāminah*. Sayda, 1967, pp. 7–19.

————. "Transitions in Arabic Poetry Today," *Middle East Forum*, Vol. XLIII, No. 1, 1967.

————. *al-Ḥurrīya wa-al-Tūfān*. Beirut, 1963.

Karam, Antūn Ghaṭṭās. *Muḥāḍarāt fī Jubrān Khalīl Jubrān, Sīratuhu wa-Takwīnuhu al-Thaqāfī, Muʾallafātuhu al-ʿAra-*

bīyah. Cairo, Maʿhad al-Dirāsāt al-ʿArabīyah al-ʿĀliyah, 1964.

————. *La vie et l'oeuvre de Gibran Khalīl Gibran*. Thesis, Sorbonne, 1958.

Khafājī, Muḥammad ʿAbd al-Munʿim. *al-Binā' al-Fannī li-al-Qaṣīdah al-ʿArabīyah*. Cairo, Maktabat al-Qāhirah, 1964.

al-Khāl, Yūsuf. "Qaḍāyā al-Shiʿr al-Muʿāṣir, li-Nāzik al-Malā'ikah," *Shiʿr* 24 (Fall 1962), 138–152.

Khouri, Mounah. *Poetry and the Making of Modern Egypt (1882–1922)*. Leiden, E. J. Brill, 1971.

Khulūṣī, Ṣafā'. *Fann al-Taqṭiʿ al-Shiʿrī wal-al-Qāfiyah*. 3rd ed. Beirut, 1966.

Lecerf, Jean. "Djabran Khalil Djabran et les Origines de la Prose Poétique Moderne," *Orient* 3 (1957), 7–14.

————. "Un Essai d'Analyse Fonctionelle: Les Tendances Mystiques du Poète Libanis d'Amérique Gabrān Halīl Gabrān," *Studia Islamica* I (Nov. 1963), 121–135; II (July 1954), 131–155.

Majmūʿat al-Rābiṭah al-Qalamīyah, li-Sanat 1921. Beirut, Dār Ṣādir, 1964.

al-Malā'ikah, Nāzik. *Qaḍāyā al-Shiʿr al-Muʿāṣir*. Beirut, Dar al-Ādāb, 1962.

Mandūr, Muḥammad. *al-Naqd wa-al-Nuqqād al-Muʿāṣirūn*. Cairo, Maktabat Nahḍat Miṣr, 1963 (?).

al-Maqdisī, Anīs al-Khūrī. *al-Ittijāhāt al-Adabīyah fī al-ʿĀlam al-ʿArabī al-Muʿāṣir*. 3rd rev. ed. Beirut, Dār al-ʿIlm li-al-Malāyīn, 1963.

Marsot, Afaf Lutfi al-Sayyid. "The Beginnings of Modernization among the Rectors of al-Azhar, 1798–1879," in W. R. Polk (ed.), *Beginnings of Modernization in the Middle East*, Chicago, 1968, pp. 267–280.

Moreh, S. "Blank Verse (*al-Shiʿr al-Mursal*) in Modern Arabic Literature," *Bulletin of the School of Oriental and African Studies* XXIX:3 (1966), 483–505.

————. "Free Verse (*al-Shiʿr al-Ḥurr*) in Modern Arabic Literature: Abu Shadi and His School, 1926–46," *Bulletin of the School of Oriental and African Studies* XXXI:1 (1968), 28–51.

————. "Poetry in Prose (*al-Shiʿr al-Manthūr*) in Modern Arabic Literature," *Middle Eastern Studies* IV:4 (July 1968), 330–360.

Naimy, Nadeem N. *Mikhail Naimy, an Introduction*. Beirut, American University of Beirut, 1967 (Publications of the Faculty of Arts and Sciences, Oriental Series, 47).

DATE DUE

NOV 3 0 201			

Demco, Inc. 38-293